The Girl from Botany Bay

Convicts embarking for Botany Bay by Thomas Rowlandson (1756–1827)
(by permission of the National Library of Australia)

The Girl
from
Botany Bay

Carolly Erickson

WILEY

John Wiley & Sons, Inc.

Published by John Wiley & Sons, Inc., Hoboken, New Jersey
Published simultaneously in Canada

Design and production by Navta Associates, Inc.

For general information about our other projects and services, please contact our Customer Care Department within the United States at (800) 762-2974, outside the United States at (317) 572-3993 or fax (317) 572-4002.

Wiley also publishes its books in a variety of electronic formats. Some content that appears in print may not be available in electronic books. For more information about Wiley products, visit our web site at www.wiley.com.

Library of Congress Cataloging-in-Publication Data:

Erickson, Carolly, date.
   The girl from Botany Bay / Carolly Erickson.
     p. cm.
Includes bibliographical references and index.
   ISBN 0-471-27140-3
   1. Bryant, Mary, b. 1765. 2. Thieves—England—Cornwall (County)—Biography.
3. Exiles—Australia—Botany Bay (N.S.W.)—Biography. 4. Women prisoners—
Australia—Botany Bay (N.S.W.)—Biography. 5. Penal colonies—Australia—Botany
Bay (N.S.W.)—History. I. Title.
   HV6653.B78E75   2004
   994.4'02—dc22   2003026038

Printed in the United States of America
10 9 8 7 6 5 4 3 2 1

I

A SHARP SALT wind rose off the estuary, stirring the bare branches of the trees along the riverbank and driving the gulls that swooped and dove beside the ferry toward the sodden foreshore. Passengers were disembarking from the ferry, making their way along the high road in the direction of Plymouth Dock, walking briskly against the wind and looking nervously toward the margins of the road, keeping watch for menacing characters.

The road was crowded on this raw January day in 1786, market carts trundling past, laborers headed for the hiring fair, shoppers bound for the establishments of milliners and drapers, ironmongers and tailors. Plymouth was the greatest entrepôt in the West Country; its harbor sheltered trading vessels from Virginia and the West Indies as well as France, Spain and the Netherlands. Goods in great variety were on display in its shops, and provincial travellers arriving from

Cornwall on the ferry brought with them thick purses and wallets filled with coins and notes to spend.

Ascending the road as it led up from the dock was Agnes Lakeman, a young, well-dressed woman travelling alone, clutching her cashmere shawl, the ribbons of her black silk bonnet tossed and blown by the constant wind. She wore gold rings, and a gold necklace gleamed at her throat. She walked more slowly than the other passengers leaving the ferry, and before long she had fallen behind them. Her eyes were on the uneven surface of the road. She did not notice the women approaching her until it was too late to escape them.

There were three young women, one of them tall and dark-haired, the others of average height, all robust and carrying staves, all dressed in the cheap, flashy capes, skirts and high boots of highwaywomen.

They surrounded Agnes and demanded her silk bonnet, her jewelry and other valuables. She screamed and struggled, and the tallest of the highwaywomen struck her. Terrified and in pain, Agnes handed over what her attackers demanded, and they ran off, leaving her bleeding on the road.

In time other passengers from the ferry came upon Agnes where she lay, helped her up, and heard her story. They set up a hue and cry for the three highwaywomen, who were at length discovered at a low tavern, spending some of the nearly twelve pounds they had gotten from the sale of Agnes's property. The highwaywomen were seized and turned over to the local magistrate, who locked them up in Plymouth jail.

The leader of the trio, Mary Broad, had been in jail before, but only for picking pockets and stealing fruit. She had been a mere girl then, scarcely out of childhood. Now, however, she was twenty, nearly twenty-one, and her crime was far more severe.[1] Highwaywomen were hanged, she had seen them hanged, arms pinioned behind their backs, legs tied together, nooses around their necks. She had watched them fall through the trapdoor and heard their necks snap— and sometimes, when their necks did not snap right away, she had seen their agony, their legs jerking horribly, their faces purple with engorged blood, as they slowly strangled to death.

She knew what it was to be hanged, to die, to have one's corpse displayed at the crossroads, stinking and full of corruption, in full view of passersby.

She had always known the price criminals paid for their trespass—yet she had also known, for everyone knew, that most thieves and highwaywomen and smugglers were never caught. And if they were not caught, they could not be tried or hanged. So, at fourteen, she had run away or allowed herself to be led away, far from home, into the dim protecting wildness of the forest where the outlaw bands lived.

There, at least, she had been well fed—unlike her earlier life in her parents' cottage, where food had always been scarce. In the forest, with the poachers and the runaways, the outcasts, the madmen and rebels, she had always had enough. She thought of herself as a forest dweller, one who lived outside the pale. She had chosen that life, yet it often seemed as if it had been thrust upon her, by her parents' poverty, by the widespread want in the town in which she lived, by the repeated failure of the harvest and the high taxes demanded by the king's officers.

Times were very hard, and if she and her companions Mary Haydon and Catherine Fryer could make nearly twelve pounds by robbing a fat rich farmwife on the high road, then they had a right to try. Or so Mary Broad thought as she sat, shivering, on the cold stone floor of her cell in Plymouth jail, waiting to be delivered to Exeter Assizes for her trial.

Mary's rebellious thoughts were commonplace in the West of England in 1786, for more and more villagers and townspeople were acting outside the bounds of law, putting themselves at risk of prosecution for acts of defiance. The unsettled times seemed to call for desperate measures, and women were often at the forefront of the agitation for change.

When grain prices rose, angry townsmen in Exeter sent their wives "in great numbers" to the corn market to harangue the farmers, threatening that unless prices were lowered, the women would come and take the grain by force. The farmers submitted. Only the previous year, outside the Cornish town of Bodmin, a crowd of women swarmed around a grain convoy, drove off those who were transporting the grain and carried the heavy sacks off to their villages. Famine, in their view, had its own imperatives; if the law stood in the way of the fair distribution of grain, then the law had to be flaunted.

All crime, especially theft, was on the increase—or so contemporaries believed.[2] The citizenry was thought to be increasingly "refractory to government, insolent, and tumultuous." Deference to authority was on the wane. The lower orders envied those above them, and did not hesitate to act out their resentment by violent means.

Only six years earlier, in the summer of 1780, London had been in an uproar. For seven days, from June 2 on, rioters ran amuck, stripping distilleries and imbibing their contents, ransacking armories, burning private houses, looting homes and chapels, breaking into jails and freeing prisoners to join in the unstoppable rampage. No one was safe. Terrified citizens locked themselves in their houses and barred their doors, but there was no escaping the destruction. Seventy houses were reduced to smoldering ashes, four jails went up in flames. Downing Street came under assault, as did the Bank of England. King George called out the militia, and ultimately troops fired on the mob, killing hundreds, but not before nearly nine hundred Londoners had died and many more had been left injured.

The "time of terror," which had been triggered by mass protest over a parliamentary bill ending long-standing legal restrictions against Catholics, was only the most alarming and the most prolonged in a series of riots in the capital, one every other year or so, for the past several decades. And the violence in London was paralleled by frenzied attacks in provincial areas. Skilled laborers in Nottinghamshire armed themselves and tore down factories, breaking machines and vowing not to stop until they had destroyed every mechanical device in England. Mobs set the homes of wealthy factory owners on fire. Judges' and magistrates' dwellings were attacked. Gangs threatened the peace of the streets in towns small and large, until the line between criminality and civil anarchy was blurred, and many wondered whether England would ever know settled times again.

In Mary Broad's small Cornish town of Fowey, in the year in which she was seized and jailed, the perceived crisis of lawbreaking coincided with a wider emergency. For 1786 was the year the pilchards ceased to run.

Eighteenth-century Cornwall was sustained by the pilchard harvest, the deluge of small herringlike fish that began arriving by the millions each summer and went on arriving, shoal after teeming shoal, into the fall. So abundant were the pilchards that they spilled out of overflowing nets, flopped out of full carts and bins, practically jumped out of the sea into the fishing boats. In normal years hundreds of tons of fish were caught, pressed and salted down in barrels, to be shipped to France, Spain and Italy—countries where meatless days were observed frequently and a great deal of fish was eaten during Lent—or kept for winter food. Cornish families survived the cold months by eating salted pilchards. Mariners relied on the trade in pilchards for their livelihood.

But in the summer of 1786 the fish failed to arrive. And not only were there no fish for trading or eating (Mary's family, like many others, tried to keep themselves alive by eating limpets) but there were few stores of other food. Harvests had been poor for several years, and money to import food was scarce, since in the aftermath of the American war, shipping of all kinds had been greatly reduced. Smuggling, the clandestine trade in brandy, wine, tobacco and salt that for centuries had provided additional revenue to the Cornish economy, had been curtailed by increased government vigilance and suppression efforts, and mining, the other cornerstone of solvency in the West Country, had also fallen off as the prices of copper and tin dropped.

And if the disastrous lack of fish and loss of other income sources were not enough, taxes rose: house taxes, window taxes, hat taxes, tallow and candle taxes, taxes on linen and cotton—above all salt taxes, which were so high they virtually forced the majority of the local population to obtain their salt by illegal means. It was no wonder the numbers of the poor increased so markedly, or that so many were driven by their poverty to leave their familiar haunts and occupations, unable to find new work at a living wage. Wages in the West Country were very low at the best of times, and the 1780s were among the worst of times—at least in Fowey.

Many died of malnourishment and disease. Many others emigrated. Still others, like Mary, turned to crime—and though most of them evaded capture, she was among the unlucky who did not.

So she prepared herself for her trial to come, nursing thoughts of revenge against Agnes Lakeman, dreaming of escaping back to the forest, but above all dreading, with the dread of the condemned, that before long she would be hanged until dead, and her body would be just another corpse at the crossroads, a warning to the law-abiding not to seek a life of crime.

II

*T*WO MONTHS LATER a cart bumped along the new turnpike road that led upland from Plymouth, making good time as the road was paved and its few ruts kept regularly repaired. Spring had nearly come, the forsythia were in bud, the showy flowers of the mesembryanthemum just beginning to appear among clumps of bright fleshy green leaves. As the road rose higher, beginning to skirt the edge of Dartmoor, the prisoners could glimpse the sea in the distance, its blue expanse dotted with fishing boats, its surface dimpled with ripples and the froth of breaking waves.

Immense granite boulders rose up out of the moorland, the bogs bright green and the gushing streams broad and swift after months of rain. Many hours after leaving Plymouth the cart rounded Hay Tor, and from its height, the prisoners could look across to the red cliffs of Budleigh Salterton and down into the lush estuary of Teignmouth.

But to Mary Broad, and the companions to whom she was shackled by heavy iron chains, the wide vistas, the warm sun and soft air brought scant comfort. They were dirty, hungry, thirsty, and desperately uncomfortable, and all that awaited them at the end of their journey was more dirt, hunger, thirst and misery—and then, most likely, execution.

Villagers shouted at them and threw clods of earth as they passed, even the children yelling out abuse. No shelter was provided for them during the cold night hours, no privacy, no way even to relieve themselves, as they were kept shackled. The beauties of the Exe Valley, the waterfalls, budding apple orchards, fields of wild daffodils, passed in a blur. At last the towers of Exeter Cathedral came into view, and then the roofline of the medieval guildhall, and the spires of the lesser churches. The cart trundled on toward Exeter Castle where the prisoners were taken off and led to the jail.

The Lenten Assizes opened with some ceremony, the two presiding justices, Sir James Eyre, Baron of the Court of Exchequer, and Sir Beaumont Hotham, his deputy, processing solemnly in their long black gowns, elaborate wigs and tricorn hats along Exeter High Street accompanied by the Lord Mayor, barristers, the sheriff and under-sheriff and an array of lesser dignitaries. The Quarter Sessions were an important occasion, a solemn season in the town's year. They combined pomp and the gravity of the law with the aweful spectacle of justice being done to malefactors—for at the conclusion of the sessions, those condemned to death were hanged. The townspeople expected their quota of hangings; if enough thieves, murderers, counterfeiters and embezzlers were executed, then the law was thought to be effectively combatting crime.

Sir James Eyre, in his gown and high-piled wig, was the solemn representative of none other than His Majesty George III; the justice he dispensed was the king's own justice. The assizes were called into session in the king's name, the prisoners indicted, tried and sentenced on his behalf. When Mary and her companions were ushered into the courtroom where Mr. Justice Eyre and Mr. Justice Hotham presided, they were, by extension, standing in the presence of royalty, and were expected to conduct themselves accordingly.

But the room in which they found themselves was, if contemporary accounts are to be trusted, nothing fit for royalty—rather the reverse. Courtrooms stank of the reeking clothes and infected bodies of prisoners, many of whom had "the itch"—a scabrous skin disease—and all of whom were crawling with lice. The courtroom air, one magistrate wrote, was "the most unwholesome, as well as nauseous, air in the universe."[1] At some Quarter Sessions, jail fever (typhus) carried off not only prisoners but jurymen, barristers, even judges. Spectators in the courtroom brought scented handkerchieves and bunches of flowers to hold under their noses while they watched the proceedings; when they left, they checked their coat sleeves and petticoats for fleas and lice.

When Mary's name was called she went forward to stand before the wooden frame of the bar, a strapping, dark-haired, grey-eyed young woman, five feet four inches tall, grimy but stalwart and unabashed. No doubt she looked much coarsened by life, her hands chapped and rough, her speech raw and thick with the local accent of Fowey, her complexion reddened from drink and exposure to the sun and the stinging Cornish wind.

The clerk who took down the bare details of Mary's court appearance did not record anything of her truculent stoicism as she faced Justice Eyre and his black-robed colleagues. Her accusation was read out: that she did "feloniously assault Agnes Lakeman, spinster, on the King's Highway, putting her to corporeal fear and danger of her life" and that she stole, "violently," a silk bonnet and other goods worth eleven pounds eleven shillings. The judges were stern, the law unforgiving. Mary Broad was sentenced to be hanged for highway robbery.

Highway robbers were noted for their nonchalance in the face of death; the most notorious of them gave banquets in prison on the night before their hangings, and went to the scaffold the following morning swaggering and grinning.[2] Mary did her best to emulate her predecessors, steeling herself not to react to the words of condemnation, remaining stalwart and outwardly unafraid, though her knees felt weak and she could not help seeking out her accomplices Catherine Fryer and Mary Haydon, who were in the courtroom with her, awaiting their own trials.

As soon as her sentence was read out, Mary was taken away and another prisoner brought to the bar.

There was a long file of prisoners coming up to stand before the bar that day, young and old, robust and withered, some demoralized, some loud and obstinate, a few broken in spirit, more calloused, annealed by years of conflict with the law. The roll call of prisoners was a melancholy one: Elizabeth Cole, who stole a few bits of pottery, Elizabeth Baker, who stole a calf skin, Susannah Handford, who was being tried posthumously for having "taken powders" to produce an abortion (the powders made her ill, and ultimately she bled to death). Most of the accused were being tried for theft, or assault, or breach of the peace.

James Martin, a tall, muscular Irishman from County Antrim, twenty-six years old, was convicted of stealing eleven heavy iron bolts from the Powderham Castle estate of his employer, Viscount Courtney.[3] The viscount being a prominent figure, the case drew local interest; when Martin was sentenced to be hanged, there may have been an audible sigh of satisfaction in the courtroom.

Nearly four hours were devoted to the trial of Thomas Ruffel, a steward accused of the murders of his master and mistress. Ruffel professed his innocence, presented witnesses in his defense and insisted that the murders were committed by another or others. But Justice Eyre and his colleagues were implacable, the evidence was against Ruffel and he was sentenced to be hanged, and afterwards to be dismembered and "anatomized."

No one expected leniency, particularly when the accused were adjudged to be guilty of crimes punishable by death—which included everything from treason and murder to shoplifting, malicious maiming of cattle and shooting at a revenue officer. Cutting down trees was punishable by execution, as was sending threatening letters or pulling down houses or counterfeiting or kidnapping an heiress.[4] It was not unheard-of for a justice to take into account the character of the accused, and the circumstances under which his or her crime was committed. But most prisoners were assumed to be "abandoned characters," incapable of amendment or moral rehabilitation, better off dead.[5] Pregnant women convicted of capital crimes could apply to be examined by a panel of matrons who might recommend that they be spared, at least until their babies were born.[6] Some judges took bribes, especially from women prisoners, offering the women liberty in exchange for "amicable visits."[7] Justice Eyre and his fellow judges seem to have been incorruptible, and the assizes took their inexorable course, with prisoner after prisoner condemned to be whipped or pilloried, to be imprisoned or, in many cases, to die.

After several days, the long list of cases having come to an end, the hangings began. The townsfolk of Exeter gathered at Heavitree to watch the executions. When Thomas Ruffel was dragged to the scaffold, struggling and shouting out great oaths, they watched—some shuddering, some laughing, some crossing themselves in superstitious fear—as he lashed out at the hangman and, failing in his efforts to free himself, swung and danced crazily at the end of the rope until he strangled.

Mary was waiting her turn, unaware that events in London were to bring about her deliverance.

In the fall of 1786 the Lords Commissioners of the Treasury ordered that a new colony was to be planted, in New South Wales, on the southeastern corner of the vast continent that the Dutch claimed under the name of New Holland—and that we now know as Australia. The English Captain Cook, traveling in the *Endeavour* with the naturalist Sir Joseph Banks, had charted the fertile east coast of the continent in 1770, and the British claimed that coast, and all the adjacent islands, in the name of King George.

The plantation of the new colony was intended not only to undergird the British claim to the land but to solve the growing problem of jail overcrowding. For well over a century it had been customary to transport British convicts to colonial areas; convict labor had been an essential element in the widening and strengthening of the empire.[8] With the outbreak of the American War of Independence, they could no longer be sent to the American colonies. New settlements had to be considered. One proposal was that a colony be started on the River Gambia, on the Atlantic coast of Africa.

A survey ship was sent out, the sloop *Nautilus*, in August of 1785, but the officers reported that the coast was dry and inhospitable. The Caffre Coast was also considered, before being rejected because the British government preferred not to risk conflict with the Dutch, who were well established there. Other locales were evaluated: Madagascar, Tristan da Cunha, Algiers, Canada, the West Indies. Entrepreneurs suggested sending convicts to work in the herring fisheries in the North Sea, or to mine coal or work in lead factories.[9] But New South Wales, despite its distance from Britain, seemed to offer the best combination of qualities—a temperate climate, inviting terrain and thousands of square miles of empty land. Virgin territory, tabula rasa, a clean slate, where prisoners could work out their years of exile while building a self-sufficient community subject to the British crown.

By the time the Easter Assizes were being held in Exeter, six transport vessels and three supply ships had been chartered and officers and crew assigned for the journey to New South Wales.

Throughout the fall and winter of 1786–1787, vessels were acquired, mariners and officers appointed, purveyors of food and supplies contracted. Only one requisite was missing: female companions for the hundreds of convicts and unmarried soldiers and officials. (An all-male community was not to be contemplated; its probable sexual vagaries would be an abomination.) At first the suggestion was made that Polynesian women could be kidnapped and brought to the new colony as companions for the men, but that tentative plan was set aside.[10] Instead, an ingenious idea was put forward, that female convicts, who were all assumed to be "abandoned" women, ought to be provided for the men, serving their sexual needs while at the same time helping to clear the overcrowded jails.

Justice Eyre and his colleagues had been ordered to choose, from among the men and women condemned to execution or prison, those who were relatively young and strong for transportation to New South Wales.[11] Sixteen were chosen, their names read out in a sonorous roll call: Thomas Watson, Anthony Mayne, James Martin the tall Irishman from County Antrim, William Coombe called "Kneebone," and so on until the final three names, Mary Haydon, Catherine Fryer and Mary Broad.

Reprieve!

When she heard her name read, all Mary's stoic defiance fell away, replaced by a puzzled hopefulness. She and the others were to be "transported beyond the seas" to an unnamed destination. They would serve out their seven-year sentences in this unknown place, and after that they would be free.

She was free now—free of the dread of death. Seven years was not such a long time, only about one-third of her life so far. In seven years she would be twenty-seven, nearly twenty-eight. Young enough to start afresh. Catherine and Mary would be going along to the new place, to serve their sentences alongside her. She would not be completely friendless there.

With some slight apprehension, mingled with a deep relief, Mary heard the clerk announce the term of her sentence. His Majesty had been graciously pleased to extend the royal mercy to her; she had been saved.

With iron shackles attached to her ankles, and chained to her fellow convicts by an iron chain, Mary Broad was put aboard a cart to be taken away. But this journey was far different from the one she had taken only a few short days before. As the cart rumbled along the high road out of Exeter, her iron bonds felt lighter, the air fresher and warmer, the newly opened flowers of the forsythia bright with color. And when they reached the edge of Dartmoor, on the high ground, she looked out eagerly toward the horizon for her first glimpse of the sea, knowing that before long a ship would be waiting in the harbor to take her to a new life.

III

THE SHACKLES FELT LIGHT—for a few hours. But by the second day of the journey the iron had begun to rub the skin of Mary's ankles raw, and with every jolt of the cart she longed for the trip to be over. At last the road dipped and they began to approach Plymouth Sound, with its maze of inlets. The broad blue extent of the Cattewater came into view, with Sutton Pool and Mill Bay and finally the Hamoaze, where a derelict ship, its masts gone, its sides covered in green slime, lay mired in a mudbank.

This was the prison ship *Dunkirk*, where the Exeter prisoners awaiting transportation were ordered to be confined.

The convicts smelled the hulk before they saw her, for she reeked of sewage and rotting ordure and the foul stench of decaying wood and unwashed humanity. Effluent from the ship was dumped onto the mudflat around her, worsening the general odor that the sharp tang of the sea air did nothing to dispel. Towering over the surrounding flats, her hull blackened with mire where the thick growth of weed and algae ended, the hulk *Dunkirk* loomed up before the approaching convicts like an apparition, a dark and spectral form around which the rising tide began to lap.

Chained to another prisoner, Mary was brought aboard, and left on deck where marine guards with drawn cutlasses looked the newcomers over—their eyes resting with particular scrutiny on the women. The guards, one inmate later wrote, were "of the lowest class of human beings, wretches devoid of all feeling, ignorant in the extreme, brutal by nature, and rendered tyrannical and cruel by the consciousness of the power they possess."[1]

Many of these marines were veterans of the American war, hardened survivors of exhausting campaigns, dispirited at the prospect of a long and difficult voyage and alert to the possibility of trouble. Only days earlier, hundreds of convicts aboard another prison ship off Portsmouth Harbor rebelled en masse and attempted to subdue their guards. The marines aboard that vessel, obeying the shouted commands of their officers, had stood their ground, fired their pistols into the yelling, frenzied mob and shot eight of the convicts dead, wounding several dozens more.

It had been a terrifying scene, berserk inmates attacking their guards with sticks of ship timber and lengths of iron from the blacksmith's shop, officers running, guards pursuing fleeing convicts who were trying to escape over the side of the ship, the wounded screaming and the air thick with smoke from the fired weapons.

The recent rebellion had been only one of many. Convicts escaped in twos and threes, sometimes half a dozen, sometimes twenty or more at a time. They broke into the captain's cabin and seized the arms chest, then, using the weapons to overpower the guards, escaped across the treacherous, quicksand-ridden mudflats or in boats brought alongside the hulks by accomplices on the outside. Some escapes were permanent, but many of the escapees were recaptured and hanged, or shot once they reached the shore. Hundreds managed to gain the safety of the forest, or to make their way to London, where they melted into the anonymity of the criminal underworld and evaded pursuit.

Once on board the *Dunkirk* Mary and her companions were warned by their warders that any attempt they might make to begin an uprising would meet with a swift and severe response, with no mercy shown. One look at the resident prisoners around them, many of whom bore terrible long red scars down their backs from floggings, or were marked by livid bruises or amputated limbs, told the newcomers that they dared not treat escape lightly.

The convict wretches who gathered to stare at the new arrivals and shout insults at them were a sorry sight indeed. Most of them had been living aboard the *Dunkirk* for many months, some for years. Their backs bent from the weight of their shackles, gaunt from malnourishment and pale as mushrooms from too little sun and air, the inhabitants of the *Dunkirk* were more like disembodied spirits than earthly creatures—though the red rash that discolored their skin and the green sputum they coughed up from their unhealthy lungs were corporeal enough. Certainly the fleas and lice that speckled their dirty shirts and narrow, emaciated chests found them worth preying upon.

The newcomers were hardly given time to take stock of their guards and their weakened companions before they were separated into two groups, the men on one side of the ship, the women on the other, and roughly stripped of every vestige of their clothing.

Mary was plunged naked into a large washtub and scrubbed. When she emerged she was handed her unwashed clothes to put on again (there being no prison garments available), her fetters were reattached and she was sent down into the dark and stinking hold of the ship.

A chorus of whistles and catcalls greeted Mary and the other newly arrived women as they descended into the murk of the hold, and saw for the first time the women with whom they were to share their captivity and make their journey.

They were filthy. The whites of their eyes were preter-naturally bright against their dirt-grimed skin, their uncombed hair was stiff with dirt, their clothes were dingy and tattered. So rank was the stench that rose from their long-unwashed bodies that it threatened to overpower the odors from the overflowing slop buckets that served them as chamberpots.

They were noisy. Raucous laughter and foul oaths assaulted Mary as she made her way, bent over so as to avoid hitting her head, along the narrow path between the bunks built into the wall. The convict women were rough-spoken, challenging, full of verbal attacks. They swore at the newcomers, at one another, at the guards and at their fate. They cheered and booed one another when fights broke out. Taunts, mockery, sneering remarks were flung in Mary's direction, the constant stridor of the women a thick wall of sound from which there seemed no escape.

They were shameless. Crammed cheek by jowl in their dozens into a space too small for half their number, they abandoned even the most rudimentary civility and modesty and undressed, relieved themselves, vomited, and engaged in coarse erotic play in public. Privacy was impossible: every act was observed, every conversation overheard. The most flamboyant of the women flaunted their thin bodies, the most aggressive of them shoved and slapped and elbowed and struck one another with energetic abandon. Every scrap of food was fought over, every inch of space contested. Emotions were raw and the worst of them elicited.

Finally, the convict women were savage. They cared only for self-preservation, or so it seemed to Mary in her first days and nights in the *Dunkirk*'s dim hold. To survive she would have to adopt their belligerent, feral behavior. She would have to become one of them, filth, noise, shamelessness and all.

The prevailing tone among the women aboard the *Dunkirk*, and prison hulks like her, was one of debased squalor. All were dragged down to the lowest level of behavior. Yet not all the prisoners were alike, either in their origins or their habits of life. In actuality, women apprehended for lawbreaking in Mary's day varied greatly from one to another in background, personality and character.

Some, to be sure, were old lags, survivors of years of prison life, card sharpers, shoplifters, swindlers and jewel thieves. Some bragged that they came from families who had been swindlers and highwaymen for many generations. A small percentage were sociopaths, not a few were mentally ill, some retarded. Most had been brought to trial for theft or prostitution, and were single women from London.[2] A very few were elderly (the elderly tended to die soon after being incarcerated). Many were driven to crime by poverty, reduced, after selling everything they owned, to stealing small items to sell for money to buy food. Others were seduced and abandoned—following which, all respectable life paths being closed to them, they survived by prostitution.

Some of the women brought to justice were victimized by

unscrupulous opportunists who used the courts to destroy them. A contemporary wrote down the story of one "timid, modest" sixteen-year-old prisoner brought before the magistrate for theft at about the same time as Mary Broad was apprehended. The sixteen-year-old's name was Mary Rose, and she was the daughter of a well-to-do farmer. Seduced by an officer who promised to marry her, Mary eloped with him to Lincoln, still unmarried, where the officer received word (or so he told his fiancée) that he had been posted abroad. Before leaving her, however, he gave the landlady of their boardinghouse a sum of money to cover the cost of Mary's lodging and meals in his absence. Whereupon the landlady, seeing a way to keep the money without having to actually provide room and board for the girl, accused Mary of stealing from her. On the strength of the criminous landlady's perjured testimony, Mary was condemned—though her family was eventually able to uncover the villainy of the landlady and bring her to justice.[3]

It was the girls from the country, like Mary Rose, who suffered most when put into prison. Many were relative innocents, vulnerable and trusting, "countrywomen in misfortune," as one observer called them. Sent aboard the prison hulks, thrown in among vulpine companions, they often failed to adapt. They kept to themselves, "pale as death," eyes red from weeping, refusing whatever meager solace might be offered by a well-meaning stranger. Before long they succumbed to their melancholy and died.

Had Mary Broad been such a girl, rather than a forest-dwelling highwaywoman, she too might have died. Instead she made a place for herself within the hulk community, adjusting as best she could to the daily regimen and falling in with the prevailing norms.

As with the other convicts, food became Mary's constant

preoccupation. Like the others she was always hungry, her stomach growling and hurting. The skimpy portions of stringy beef, ox cheek, herring and cheese served to the prisoners were often inedible, the meat or fish rotting and putrid, the bread moldy and half baked. Barley was added to the meat broth to make a much-hated dish called "smiggins," served on meatless days. The food was prepared on shore and brought out to the hulk in a boat. Waiting convicts watched the provision boat approach, smelled the food as it was hoisted aboard the *Dunkirk*, and, if it reeked, sometimes threw it back overboard—for which they were all severely flogged.[4]

One prisoner spoke for all when he summarized his reaction to the terrible rations. "Half the time they give us provisions which the very dogs refuse," he wrote. "Half the time the bread is not baked, and is only good to bang against a wall. The meat looks as though it had been dragged in the mud for miles. Twice a week we get putrid salt fish, that is to say, herrings on Wednesday and cod on Friday."[5]

Hunger drove Mary and her fellow prisoners to eat what they were served—less a bite or two set aside to share with those unfortunates who, having tried to escape, were put on two-thirds rations. But some of the food they simply could not bring themselves to swallow, and it was thrown onto the refuse heap on the mudflat or given to the pigs.

Constant hunger made the prisoners highly susceptible to disease, and they succumbed, in large numbers, to typhus, pneumonia, dysentery, smallpox and tuberculosis. Infection bred in the ship's clogged drains ahead and astern, and in the stagnant ponds, and in the mounds of garbage that heaped higher and higher the longer the *Dunkirk* lay moored in the mudbank.

Every night more convicts died of disease—causing an

immediate scramble for the deceased's clothes and other meager possessions. Corpses were tossed out of their bunks so that the narrow space belonging to them could be ransacked. In the morning the dead bodies were wheeled to the dead house on deck, then buried in shallow graves in the marshes near the ship.[6] Besides disease, murder and suicide, the major cause of death was the "universal depression of spirits" noticed by one visitor to the hulks, a depression that attacked even the hardiest inmates from time to time. Overall, one in every three prisoners died aboard the *Dunkirk*—but every evening new prisoners arrived to take the places of those who had passed away.[7]

So many died—but Mary survived, despite the scant food and epidemics, the nights of broken sleep, the lack of fresh air (the portholes and hatches on the shore side of the *Dunkirk* were kept closed, lest the rank odor from the ship offend the citizens of Plymouth) and the shortage of water. She became accustomed to the noise of the creaking timbers, the clank and rattle of chains, the din and uproar of shouted oaths and harsh orders, the sharp pain of being elbowed in the ribs and the habit of elbowing back. She adjusted to the brutality of the guards, who beat recalcitrant prisoners insensible with heavy sticks, and to the carousing officers, many of whom were very drunk by ten in the morning, and some of whom were sadists. She even grew used to the casual public sodomy among the men, and to the rough lovemaking that went on between the men and women—lovemaking in which she joined—the iron screen meant to keep the genders apart being ineffectual.

Much furtive sex went on, along with fighting, gambling, and the plotting of escapes, during the long nights when the guards left the convicts on their own, locked belowdecks. The hatches were closed, mob rule prevailed. Some of the men occupied themselves in hammering crowns and half crowns into counterfeit sixpences. Others carved inkstands out of pieces of ox bone to sell in the nearby town. A few tried to read, or improve their minds by learning mathematics or languages. But these were the ridiculed minority: most of the convicts lounged, swore, played cards and dice, fought, and seduced or raped one another.

On such a night in December of 1786, Mary Broad became pregnant, by a man named Spence.

IV

ELEVEN SHIPS rode at anchor in the wide roadstead at Spithead, idling there under the warm spring sun, waiting for a favorable wind.

There were six transport vessels, square-rigged, blunt-nosed, round-bodied, heavy-timbered merchantmen of small tonnage lying low in the water, overladen with convicts. The largest of the transports, the *Alexander*, was 114 feet long and 31 feet wide, and of 452 tons; the smallest, the *Friendship*, was of 278 tons. The other four were the 345-ton, three-masted *Charlotte*, the capacious *Scarborough* and *Lady Penrhyn*, and the smaller *Prince of Wales*.[1]

The flagship of the small fleet, the ship-of-war *Sirius*, sleek and trim, towered over the squat merchantmen, her tall masts rising to fifty feet or more, while the three supply ships *Borrowdale*, *Golden Grove* and *Fishburn*, and the tender *Supply*, an old brig-rigged sloop, bobbed in the waves, junior members of the fleet. Nearby was the *Hyena*, the twenty-four-gun frigate that would escort the fleet out of the harbor and stay with it for the first week of its long journey, until it came safely past the Scilly Isles.

All the ships except the *Hyena* had been waiting nearly two months in the roadstead for the day of departure, taking aboard crew and stores, supplies and equipment, and waiting for good weather. The contractors hired to provide the many essentials for the voyage—food, live animals, coals, wood, clothing, extra ropes and spare sails, platters, pots, brooms and swabs, casks, blankets—had been late in delivering them. Even now, on the eve of departure, launches came back and forth from the shore to the vessels waiting at anchor in the roads, ferrying supplies.

The convoy was bound for New South Wales, the transports carrying some seven hundred and fifty convicts, nearly two hundred of them women. An equal number of crew members, merchant seamen, naval ratings and officers and marines, plus twenty-eight of the marines' wives and seventeen of their children, made up the total of nearly fifteen hundred aboard.

The commander of the fleet, Governor Arthur Phillip, was troubled about the coming voyage. He knew the hazards of such a lengthy journey—fifteen thousand miles—and the challenges to navigation and seamanship that it would present. Phillip was an experienced captain with long service in both the English and Portuguese navies, and had been at sea for most of his forty-eight years. He trusted his abilities. But there were serious impediments to the success of the voyage, and now, as the final day of preparation arrived, he was forced to concede that there was nothing more he could do to correct them. He had written letter after letter to the Navy Board, asking that the many defects he was aware of be remedied and warning of disaster if they were not. But his letters had not produced results, and in exasperation, he had gone on record as declining any responsibility for any deaths that might occur because of inadequate preparation and insufficient food and equipment.[2]

There were so many deficiencies. The transport ships were overcrowded and inadequately provisioned. There was not enough bread, no lime juice for the convicts to drink or sauerkraut for them to eat to prevent scurvy, no adequate regulation prison clothing for the convicts. Contractors had delivered hundreds of prison suits for the men, but they were all of the same size. The boots they supplied were adequate for land use, but fell apart when wet. Hammocks provided for sleeping were so flimsy the men fell through them on first use, and the thin, cheaply woven blankets delivered to the ships gave no warmth.[3]

The plight of the women convicts was particularly acute, and Phillip was sensitive to it. Prison clothing had been ordered for them, but was not complete by the day of embarkation. The women still wore the clothes in which they had been brought to trial, ragged and dingy after many months aboard the prison hulks.[4] Phillip complained to the Navy Board about their inadequate concern for the health of the women, many of whom were ill, and a number of whom, including Mary Broad, were pregnant. An epidemic had broken out among the women of the *Lady Penrhyn*, and there were other ongoing medical emergencies.

The commander was concerned that his Surgeon-General John White, the youngest and ablest of the ship's surgeons, might desert his post in frustration at the lack of antiscorbutics and medicines, the unhygienic conditions resulting from overcrowding, the lack of proper oversight of the convicts' living conditions. During the two months that Surgeon

White had been attending the convicts, marines and seamen in port, sixteen convicts aboard the *Alexander* had died, and a contagious mumpslike disease had broken out and was spreading throughout the fleet. There were rumors of a terrible outbreak of "ship's fever"—typhus—that White had had to refute. Phillip had done all he could to satisfy White, ordering the *Alexander* cleaned and whitewashed and painted with creosote—White's sovereign remedy against epidemics—and whitewashing the beams and sides of the ships to prevent the "unwholesome dampness" the surgeon-general detected there. But the much-needed medicines and preventives had not been delivered, and the commander was aware that his sensitive and humane principal medical officer might resign his post rather than face the certainty of more needless disease and death among his hundreds of patients. And if he resigned, he could not easily be replaced in a short time.

In the meantime the commander had other, more immediate concerns. The supply of fresh water, drawn from the noxious Thames, was unhealthy and would soon become undrinkable. Each of the ships in the fleet had been fitted out with a primitive water-freshening device called an Osbridge's machine, operated by hand, which forced the foul water through a collander-like sieve, reducing it to "numberless drops," as proponents of the machine explained, "which being exposed in this form to the open air is deprived of its offensive quality."[5] Phillip was dubious about the effectiveness of the sweetening machine, and planned to take on more fresh water in Tenerife. On further stretches of the voyage, however, there were bound to be weeks, perhaps a month or more, without any fresh water except rainwater, and this worried him.

As did the extreme shortage of ammunition for the

marines. There was only enough ammunition to provide for "immediate service," not for the entire voyage. The defect was an oversight, the result of neglect and incompetence.[6] So far the shortage of ammunition had been kept as a closely guarded secret, but in the event of a convict rebellion—something Phillip and his officers considered quite likely to happen—the marines would be vulnerable. Aboard the *Alexander*, there were only thirty-five marines to guard 213 male convicts; aboard the *Scarborough*, only thirty-three marines to guard 208 unruly, desperate men. Only adequate firepower could prevent mutiny.

Having failed in all his appeals to the Navy Board, and with the sailing season advancing, Commander Phillip decided to embark. So, with misgivings, on the afternoon of May 12, 1787, with a fresh wind rising, he gave orders for the fleet to weigh anchor and set sail.

The orders were not heeded.

The seamen, many of whom had been drinking, refused to man the capstans or go aloft until they were given the seven months of back pay they were owed, and allowed one final trip ashore to buy what they needed for the long voyage.[7]

Commander Phillip managed to deal with the emergency, sending his second lieutenant on the *Sirius,* Lieutenant King, to settle affairs forcibly, no doubt threatening the rebellious crew members with irons and the lash—and within a few hours the seamen were beginning the arduous tasks of hauling in the heavy, slime-covered anchor cables and climbing the rigging to set the sails.[8] The eleven ships of the fleet and their *Hyena* escort began to move slowly out to sea. A brisk wind from the southeast filled their sails as they moved, in the early hours of May 13, 1787, out of the roadstead and past the Isle of Wight.

Mary Broad, aboard the *Charlotte* transport with nineteen other convict women and some eighty-eight male prisoners, heard the anchor cables being hauled in and felt the rocking of the swell as the wind filled the *Charlotte*'s sails. She was five months pregnant, and the motion of the ship made her nauseous. To be sure, she was often nauseous; the smell of bad food, the reek of the ship made her stomach churn and heave.

She had not aborted the child when her menses stopped and she suspected her condition—or, at any rate, she had not succeeded in aborting it. Nothing is known of her relationship with the baby's father, the mysterious Mr. Spence: whether he was a fellow convict or a guard or an officer, whether he and Mary were affectionate lovers, or whether he raped her, or whether they coupled casually, in the dark of the hold, in a momentary assuaging of mutual lust.[9] Mary may have offered sex to Spence in return for an extra ration of food, or to avoid a beating—or to prevent being locked in the Black Hole, the lightless, all but airless cell at the bottom of the *Dunkirk*, full of rats and roaches, to which the most unfortunate of the prisoners aboard the hulk were sent for punishment.

Whatever the circumstances under which Mary's child was conceived, or whatever her feelings toward its father, she continued to carry the baby, her rounded belly prominent under her ragged gown. Spence may or may not have been aboard the *Charlotte*, but there were several other men whom Mary had known on the *Dunkirk* who were now her sailing companions on the *Charlotte*. There was James Martin, the black-haired Irishman from County Antrim who had been convicted along with Mary at the Exeter Assizes, and James Cox, a daring, aggressive convict who was in the third year of his life sentence. William Bryant, a Cornishman and a smuggler, also in the third year of his sentence (his crime had been assaulting a revenue officer), must have come to know Mary in the course of his daily duties. He was entrusted with the job of giving out provisions at mealtimes; he was to play a prominent part in Mary's story. Bryant, Cox and Martin were most likely similar in appearance to the "many fine young fellows" whom the prison reformer John Howard observed when he went aboard the *Dunkirk* a few years earlier, in 1783, made thin by their scant meals, but otherwise able-bodied.

The nineteen women who were Mary's constant companions ranged from London streetwalkers to thieves, shoplifters and receivers of stolen goods. No doubt there were a few country girls among the group, well behaved and modest, who tried to keep to themselves and avoid contact with the rougher convicts. But most of the women were "females of daring habits," experienced in crime and somewhat inured to the hardships of prison life. Not a few of the women were pregnant, or became pregnant during the course of the voyage. Some had babies at the breast. One or two may have been quite elderly, like the eighty-two-year-old woman on the *Lady Penrhyn* who was dying of dropsy when she came aboard and did not live long into the voyage.[10]

Mary and her fellow convicts were in poor health, shivering with cold at night (it had been an exceptionally cold, wet and rainy spring), handcuffed together and confined to the gloom belowdecks, suffering with colds and with chilblains on their hands. Some had frostbitten toes. Using sex as barter, they slept with the seamen, enduring the punishments subsequently doled out to them for prostitution, trying to break into the wine stores (perhaps with the seamen's help) and open the casks of porter.

Loud and obstreperous, rebellious when chastised, the

women invited further punishment. While being flogged they shouted abuse, while having iron fetters attached to their wrists they cursed and yelled out insults.[11]

They were incorrigible. Even when shut in "the box," a narrow cubicle on deck, a wooden straitjacket that kept the prisoner standing, painfully, for hours, they "wailed so loudly, and used their tongues so freely," one of the officers wrote, "that it was found necessary to place a cistern of water on the top of the box." Only when drenched were the women temporarily silent.

A punishment the women convicts particularly hated was having their heads shaved. Whipping with rope on the arms and legs was less efficacious, as was the barrel torment. Holes were cut in the top and sides of an empty flour barrel, then the barrel was dropped over the prisoner, her head and arms sticking out. Like the box, the barrel prevented lying down or sitting, and was very painful. But it did not prevent shrill tirades. Marine guards, weary of the women's tongue-lashings, tended to confine them in the dark of the coalhole, where they were served only bread and water.

Five or six days out from Spithead, the marine officers aboard the *Scarborough* detected and forestalled a mutiny. Two convicts, both experienced seamen, had attempted to organize the two-hundred-plus prisoners on board to take over the ship, planning to overpower the thirty-three marines on board (some of whom were ill) and to coerce the seamen into cooperating.[12] With supplies of ammunition pitifully low, the marines must have been both alarmed that a mutiny had been fomented and immensely relieved that it had been prevented. The two convicts who had been the organizers were hauled aboard the *Sirius* and given twenty-four lashes each by the boatswain's mate, as an example and a warning.[13]

Mary must have known of the attempted mutiny; news

of it would have spread rapidly through the fleet. Like most of the prisoners, she was probably acutely seasick during the early weeks of the voyage, when the seas ran so high Commander Phillip could not sit down to write his log and the *Charlotte* was pitched and tossed dreadfully. After a week Mary and her companions were released from their shackles and allowed on deck, but she may have been too ill to take advantage of this relative freedom. Dozens of prisoners were ill—though the mysterious mumpslike disease Surgeon White had been treating before the fleet sailed had receded, those who had come down with it responding to a dose of an emetic—and eight had died in the early days of the journey. In the third week the lookouts sighted a hillock on the horizon, and watched it rise slowly out of the sea. It was the ten-thousand-foot peak on Tenerife, the first visible landfall of the Canary Islands.

The fleet anchored in the Santa Cruz roads, opposite the jagged black rocks that erupted in erratic piles at the coastline. A boat was sent ashore for fresh water, meat and vegetables. The convicts were apprehensive. The great peak, it was said, was a mountain of fire, spewing out hot molten rock that at any moment might come pouring down the mountain's flanks and into the sea. The air was hot, the southerly wind blowing up from Africa very warm and dry. A tropical sun blazed overhead, and set rapidly in the evening, with no lingering twilight. The ocean was not the opaque, roiling, midnight blue of the Cornish coast but a heavenly azure, clear enough, at ten fathoms, to allow Mary to look down into its depths.

On one warm night, while some of the convicts from the *Alexander* were engaged in loading casks full of fresh water, one of them slipped unobserved into a small boat lying alongside the transport and got away.

He was not immediately missed, and had time to search for a means to get away from the island. Among the many ships in the harbor was a Dutch East Indiaman, an immense vessel requiring a large crew. The convict, John Powell, put himself forward as a seaman looking for a berth, and approached the first crew members he encountered. His dress, or something in his demeanor, made them wary; even though the ship was undermanned, they offered him no berth.

Unwilling to arouse suspicion, Powell let his boat drift until he was driven onto a small island in the harbor. He took shelter there, but left the boat and oars on the shore, there being no means of concealing them other than to try to sink the boat, which he was unwilling to do. The following morning a search party, seeing the boat, captured Powell and returned him to the *Sirius*.

Like the thwarted mutiny, the abortive escape of John Powell soon became notorious. Powell was put in irons, and punished. But his daring made him a hero to the other convicts, and his cleverness soon helped him to avoid the unpleasant aftereffects of his brief attempt at liberation. Knowing Commander Phillip to be just and compassionate, Powell appealed to his kindness. He managed to have a petition drawn up on his behalf, and delivered to the commander. Phillip relented, released Powell from his shackles and confinement, and let him take his place again among the other convicts.[14]

Escape! The thought of it gnawed at the convicts, monopolized their conversations, invaded their dreams. John Powell had very nearly gotten away. It was possible. Sooner or later some bold individual or group would succeed. It was only a matter of time—and opportunity. Meanwhile they had to survive, and the news from Tenerife was not good. It was early in the growing season on the island. There were very few vegetables to harvest, besides onions, and no fruit at all. Boats sent ashore came back nearly empty. There would be no fresh greens or citrus on the long, hot, hungry journey to Rio, a journey of several months. All the ships had their share of sick, and the sickness could hardly be combatted without healthful, plentiful rations. On board the *Charlotte*, among Mary's fellow convicts, fifteen were ill, one near death.

Dark squalls marched across the ocean, rank on rank, on June 10, 1787, the day the fleet weighed anchor for the voyage across the Atlantic, and a blazing sun scorched the parched, rocky hills of Tenerife. There was little wind. With the others, Mary was called to the deck of the *Charlotte* for the funeral of the second convict to die in four days.

Mary was six months pregnant now, and it was becoming more difficult, with the added bulk of her growing belly, to keep her balance amid the constant movement of the ship. Waves slapped against the hull as the chaplain read the funeral service and the corpse, covered in a shroud made from a shredded sail, was tipped overboard to sink into the azure depths. Afterwards Mary made her way, a little unsteadily, down the companionway into the hold as the fleet sailed on westward, avoiding the calms to be encountered on the African coast, into the hot latitudes, headed for the equator and points south.

V

*T*HE SEA WAS LUMINOUS.

A sheet of faint opalescent light coated its calm surface, bringing with it an eerie quiet. No swells thudded against the creaking hulls, no clangs and rattles came from the rigging. The sails hung slack, with only an occasional breeze to belly them out and move the sluggish vessels forward.

Swept southwestward by the current, the fleet sailed on, the *Sirius*, *Alexander*, *Scarborough* and *Friendship* in the lead, the *Charlotte* and *Lady Penrhyn* lagging farther and farther behind, as they sailed poorly in light winds. By day the vessels kept track of one another by shooting off their heavy guns periodically. By night the *Sirius* mounted a bright light in her tall maintop, visible for miles as a beacon to the sternmost vessels. Lanterns hung from the rigging and along the deck of all the ships cast pools of reflected light on the still water, drawing schools of flying fish that arced over the deck to fling themselves against the sails. In the morning the crew found hundreds of the tiny winged corpses, and took them to the cook.

Down through the tropics, past the Cape Verdes, the *Sirius* and her following vessels sailed, through long hot days, the heat intensified rather than relieved by heavy rains and lightning storms. Schools of blue bonitos, their silver sides gleaming, flashed just beneath the surface, blue and black pilot fish surrounded the vessels, and porpoises leapt and dove in their wakes. Whales spouted, sharks appeared, some six feet long, and the crew and officers caught them with barbed hooks hung from long poles. The *Charlotte*'s boatswain caught sixteen bonitos one day; dolphins and sharks were also hooked and brought on board.

Apart from an occasional passing ship, the convoy encountered nothing of interest. It was as if the ships had embarked on a vast watery emptiness, devoid of singularities, wide and flat, stretching away on all sides toward an infinite horizon.

Having little else to do, after completing their daily tasks of taking sights from the sun, writing the ship's log and marking their positions on the chart, noting the condition of foodstuffs and the supply of water, the crew fished and dozed and socialized. At the Tropic of Cancer, they carried out the ceremony usually observed when crossing the equator, "sluicing and ducking" all those on board who had never before passed the latitude, frolicking so lustily under the aegis of Neptune (complete with trident, long robe and false beard) that two of the ships, the *Charlotte* and the *Lady Penrhyn*, nearly ran into one another.[1]

The wind had fallen light. Thunderstorms dumped

quantities of warm rain on the ships, which seemed to inch forward, as if held back by the thick sultry air. After a day or two no wind stirred and the vessels floated, dreamlike, on the flat still pool of the sea. Heat rose in shimmering waves off the calm waters, the decks of the ships baked in the sun and became too hot to walk on. Convicts, crew and marines sweltered in the humid, steaming air, bathed in sweat, unable even to sleep, so close and stifling was the atmosphere.

Crowded with her fellow convicts in the nearly airless hold, Mary could do little but sit on her hard berth and think about water. Cool water, water overflowing in abundance, water to wash over her and assuage the thirst caused by the unbearable heat. What water she was given, carefully measured out, three quarts a day, was warm, stank, and tasted foul. As water in the casks, filled on Tenerife, began to run low, the bottoms of the casks became coated with a black fungal growth, malodorous and repellent; they yielded a soupy, cloudy, reeking liquid that bore little resemblance to the water from a clear flowing stream. She drank what was given to her, gratefully, but it nearly made her gag. Moments later her thirst returned.

All her senses were assaulted, her sense of smell most rudely. The stench of the water she drank was all but overpowered by the stink of the bilge. The great heat made the rotting food, human waste and other organic matter in the bilge water putrefy at an increased pace, and as it decomposed, it sent into the stale air exhalations beyond description.

Sitting on her berth, Mary felt her baby kick. In another two or three months, she had calculated, the child would be born. How would she manage, on scant rations and too little water, with a newborn to care for? The voyage had been hard on the babies born to convict women. Most had died.

Hers might well die—and she herself might die, as so many women did, in the aftermath of childbirth.

Dark thoughts such as these must have preyed on Mary as, day after blistering day, the terrible calm continued, the deck burning in the merciless sun so that the pitch caulking its seams melted and began to drop on the heads of the convicts in searing black chunks, scalding their flesh.[2] At night there was no relief, only more heat, sweat, and heavy air, thick and oppressive.

Rats, roaches, lice, nits, fleas, bugs of every sort plagued the convicts, marines and crew. They crawled out from the timbers of the ship, flew in dense clouds through the heavy air, landing on exposed skin and biting, nesting, infesting. Surgeon White ordered creosote applied to the convicts' area and the quarters of the marines and crew three times a week, had gunpowder exploded in the living quarters between the decks, and went about the ship himself applying liberal amounts of oil and tar and a solution of quicklime in boiling water. But for every bug or rat that was killed, a hundred more seemed to emerge, unscathed by any efforts at fumigation. And the heat bred other plagues: angry red rashes that appeared on the convicts' arms and legs, necks and chests, the rot that bred in their mouths, making teeth fall out and gums turn black, headaches that no medicine could relieve and painful boils and blisters. Many of the women fainted, their fainting fits leading to convulsions.[3] One of the women convicts, made desperate by thirst, went off her head and drank a harsh chemical, sublimate of mercury. Amazingly, she recovered from its effects.

As rations began to run low, all the live geese, chickens and pigs having been eaten and the ship's stores rotting in the excessive heat, Mary's apprehension must have grown. Would she and the others die here, in the midst of the glassy sea? Would the wind ever rise again? She drank the foul water and ate her share of the bony, dry flying fish the cook prepared, her skin itching and her baby kicking, praying for relief from the torments of the doldrums.

Accidents began to curse the fleet. Sails split or shredded and had to be replaced, one of the store ships, the *Golden Grove*, lost a mast three times and another, the *Borrowdale*, underwent a similar mishap. On the *Alexander*, one evening, a seaman who was taking in a sail fell overboard and sank before a longboat could rescue him. On a night of heavy seas, the cookhouse on the *Friendship* was swept overboard, pots, pans, trenchers, roasting spits and all. A sixty-year-old woman convict aboard the *Lady Penrhyn* fell down the steerage companionway and broke two ribs. And another convict on the *Prince of Wales*, Jane Bonner, had the misfortune to be standing in the way when a longboat got loose and rammed her against the side of the ship. It was nearly dark when the accident happened, and although Surgeon White was summoned, he could not take the risk of going in a longboat from the *Charlotte* to the *Prince of Wales*, visibility being so low. He waited until morning, by which time Jane Bonner had died.[4]

On the night of July 22, three marines bribed a sentinel and entered the hold where the women convicts were. All three were caught and court-martialled, one receiving three hundred lashes, another a hundred lashes as punishment. The incident was one of many. With the doldrums and the onset of accidents came disorders, unrest, suicide attempts (punished with flogging or solitary confinement), violations of orders and an edgy irritation that affected crew and convicts alike and led to outbreaks of violence. A marine on the *Prince of Wales* got drunk, quarreled with some of his fellow soldiers and then jumped down the main hatchway, happening to land on the wife of an officer. On Mary's ship the *Charlotte*, a marine was whipped for "unsoldierlike behavior," and the regular Saturday night drinking parties for marines and officers, captains and surgeons became ungovernable free-for-alls, with loud and abusive arguments breaking out and the men accusing one another of loutish behavior. Convicts plotted mutinies, stole scraps of metal—pots, iron hinges, brass instruments, belt buckles, pewter spoons—from which to make weapons, and manufactured counterfeit coins to use once they escaped.[5]

The longer the tedious and miserably uncomfortable voyage became, the more the convicts sank into depression and felt the need of a reason to live; for many, that reason was the dream and hope of revenge against the brutal officers and guards who treated them with rude contempt and carried huge sticks with which to beat them.[6]

Quarrels broke out between the ships' masters and the surgeons, whom the masters habitually abused, and between the officers and the naval agent, the agent wanting to accomplish the voyage as rapidly as possible, the officers hoping to spare their ships and men and allow for long layovers in port. There were endless clashes over how much sail to carry, especially after the winds began to rise at the end of July, and over whether to tack in a squall—which the merchantmen generally did—or to head into the wind with lots of sail out, as was the naval custom at the time. The convoy had already lost a good deal of canvas through sails being blown off the yards and masts lost. With the strongest winds yet to come in the high southern latitudes, squabbles grew more vehement over the need for caution versus the temptation to try to complete the voyage in record time.

Over the long weeks of cramped, wretched sailing friendships corroded and even the most congenial shipmates tended to become irritable with one another. Surgeon White developed a toxic grudge against his assistant Surgeon Balmain. Crew members fought over insignificant incidents. There was tension aboard all the vessels, made worse by drink and by the illness and fear induced by heavy seas that battered at the ships late in July.

Amid the turmoil, it was the convicts who suffered most, and who most rejoiced when at last word was spread through the fleet that a lookout aboard the *Supply* had sighted land.

The cry "Land ho!" rang out at midafternoon on August 2, and on the following day, through the haze, the high eminence of Sugar Loaf could be glimpsed rising over the harbor of Rio de Janeiro.

For four weeks the convoy lay at anchor in the busy harbor, while Commander Phillip and his officers were honored and entertained by the Portuguese port officials and the ships were repaired and made ready for the most challenging part of the voyage. Cabbages, yams, bananas, guavas, lettuce, tropical fruit in abundance were brought on board, along with stringy beef and thin chickens. The water casks were filled and sweetened, and some of the sick convicts, fed on fresh rations, began to recover.

Relieved not to have to endure the constant motion of the ship, Mary rested, perhaps hoping that her baby would be born while in port. She was in her final month, and getting around was difficult. The weather was cool, the sky mostly clear. But by the time the convoy got under way again on September 4, the stormy weather typical of the South Atlantic tossed the vessels about on high seas, and water sloshed into the hold, washing Mary and the other convict women aboard the *Charlotte* out of their berths and making them ill.

Rain was beating at the *Charlotte* on the morning of September 8 when Mary went into labor. Her pains continued throughout the dark day until, toward four in the afternoon, her baby was born.

"On the evening of the eighth, between the hour of three and four, Mary Broad, a convict, was delivered of a fine girl," Surgeon White noted in his journal.[7] Mother and child lay on the hard planks in the dark wet hold, while the rain pounded against the deck and waves slapped noisily and insistently against the hull. Presently Mary could hear, over the sounds of rain and water, the cries of the mariners as they mounted the rigging to take in the sails for the night. With the canvas trimmed, the motion of the ship lessened; a gentler rocking replaced the heaving pitch and roll, almost, the new mother may have imagined, the rocking of a cradle.

Mary had decided to call her daughter Charlotte, after the ship—and the queen. She would also have her father's name, Spence, for a record of paternity had to be kept for every child born to a female convict. Little Charlotte was a healthy baby, with a lusty cry, well made and strong. She did not appear to have suffered from being carried for nine months aboard a prison hulk and a convict transport.

Holding her baby in her arms, Mary slept, lulled by the rocking motion of the ship, the beating of the rain, the sighing and whistling of the wind, as the *Charlotte* moved out at speed and began to run down her eastings, headed for Cape Town.

VI

OR THE NEXT four months Mary and Charlotte
could not seem to get dry. The ship flew through
the choppy seas, impelled by fresh gales that bellied
out the sails until they were as taut as drumskins, and a
constant shower of salt spray shot over the bow, across the
deck and into the hold. Squalls dumped sheets of drenching
rain on the convoy, high seas washed over the decks and on
the few clear days the air was so thick with dampness that
green slime formed on the walls and the berths were slick
with moisture. Seamen aboard the *Charlotte* closed the
hatches to prevent more water coming in, but it was too
late. The convicts were soaked to the skin, their flimsy, tattered clothes clinging to their thin bodies, their outworn
shoes in pieces.

The *Charlotte* lumbered crazily in the troughs of the
waves, constantly heeling over, in danger of overturning

when she came into the wind or encountered a strong following sea. Water sloshed over every surface, soaking the light blankets allotted to the convicts, spoiling the provisions, pouring over the chests of stores and ammunition and leaving behind small fish and seaweed and the smell of salt and decay.

With the constant wet came constant cold. Although spring had come to the south latitudes, it was no mild, warm English spring but a rainy, stormy spring that gave way to an even more rainy summer. The fresh winds that drove the ships forward at high speed were chill winds, biting and raw; the convicts shivered in their light garments, especially the women, whose "nearly naked" state so disturbed Commander Phillip that while in Rio he brought aboard burlap sacks with which to make them clothes. Burlap provided little warmth, however, even when worn in layers. Whether the surgeons, who cut up sheets and blankets to make extra shirts and trousers for the male convicts, also made garments for the women is not known. The supply of clothing had been diminished when high winds blew drying laundry overboard—one of the convicts, William Brown, fell overboard and was lost while trying to retrieve his laundry from the bowsprit—and by the effects of hard wear over many months. What were needed were warm flannel shirts, flannel petticoats, woollen coats and cloaks, plus warm gloves and mittens and caps and bonnets to keep out the rain and damp. But there was no benefactor to provide these, and so day after day, as the ships drove southward, the cold became more penetrating and the seas more boisterous.

Even while anchored in Table Bay, where the convoy stayed for a month between mid-October and mid-November taking on water and provisions, there was no escape from the frigid winds, for a gale struck the ships and once the journey was resumed the sea was littered with icebergs.

Fresh challenges met the fleet as it sailed on through the cold, choppy waters, several of the ships listing badly, all heavily laden, having taken on some five hundred live animals for the long haul between the Cape and Botany Bay. Fog often shrouded the sea, reducing visibility to as little as half a mile and making the dangerous icebergs hard to avoid. They loomed up suddenly, high rocks of dirty ice, a menace to navigation for their vast submerged portions contained thrusting sharp ledges of ice that could tear out a ship's bow within seconds and send her to the bottom within minutes. The air was raw with frost, and the seamen, their fingers stiff and all but frozen, were clumsy and slow in setting the sails, the cold making the knots in the gaskets rigid.

Toward the middle of November an epidemic of dysentery began spreading, especially on the *Charlotte* where at least thirty people, including Surgeon White, were ill. The sufferers were doubled over with terrible stabbing pain in the bowels, high fever and, in the worst cases, delirium. Dark, gloomy weather and heavy seas seemed to accentuate the misery of the sick as the vessels labored on, rolling uncontrollably with waves breaking over them and the ships' pumps barely able to keep pace with the rising water below deck. Superstitious seamen cursed and crossed themselves when albatrosses, thought to be omens of delay and disaster, appeared among the petrels and gannets and Mother Carey's chickens in the cloudy sky.

Whether or not Mary and her baby daughter were afflicted with dysentery is not recorded, but by mid-December both must have been excessively thin and pale, desperately cold and in constant misery from the severe pitching and rolling of the *Charlotte*. Their water ration had been reduced to three pints a day, there was no fresh food left and the sheep, hogs and chickens were dying, their piteous bleating, squealing and clucking a wrenching counterpoint to the noise of the waves beating savagely against the ships' sides and the rattle of the rigging and the convicts' shackles. With each day more dead livestock were thrown overboard. The sailors whispered that the albatrosses had brought bad luck and that almost immediately after the birds were sighted a Norwegian sailor aboard the *Prince of Wales* had fallen overboard, the convoy traveling at such high speed that he could not be rescued.

Now the disease the sailors dreaded most, scurvy, began to make its appearance, striking the convict women first. Their gums became swollen and tender, and turned black and hard and very painful. Teeth fell out, eating became impossible. In the worst cases the victims suffered from pains in the legs and chest, with a debilitating fever. Efforts were made to prevent the scurvy from spreading; decks were washed with vinegar and smoked with brimstone. But with the constant flying spray and the sloshing of water along the decks and in the hold, such attempts at improving hygiene were pitifully feeble, and soon the scurvy spread to the crew, some of whom became too weak to go aloft. Through much of December the *Charlotte* and her companion vessels were tossed and tumbled on the often mountainous seas, seemingly directionless, at the mercy of the winds and currents, while the fearsome albatrosses, birds of ill omen, soared above them, dark wings spread wide. Meanwhile the officers, swathed in layers of flannel waistcoats and thick wool greatcoats, calculated how long the putrid water in the casks would last and whether they would make landfall before the remaining food stores gave out.

Despite all, they were making good time. The ships were covering more than a hundred miles a day, running down the Roaring Forties, the near-arctic latitudes where, at the height of the December-January antipodean summer, high winds gusted lustily and often reached gale force.[1]

Just before Christmas a fair wind blew, breaking the pattern of the extreme cold, and on Christmas Day the convicts received a slightly fuller ration than usual. "We complied, as far as was in our power, with the good old English custom," wrote the Judge Advocate David Collins, "and partook of a better dinner this day than usual; but the weather was too rough to admit much social enjoyment."[2]

There was high excitement when, through thick sheets of rain, a lookout cried "Land ho!" having sighted the outline of the coast of Van Diemen's Land (Tasmania).[3] They had been at sea nearly eight weeks, their longest stretch without making port or even sighting land from a distance.

Clutching Charlotte, now nearly four months old, Mary felt the surge of relief and joy that swept over all the ships, and joined in the weeping, singing and shouting that rose from vessel to vessel. Guns boomed, boatswain's whistles were piped, seamen danced crazily in celebration. No doubt Commander Phillip breathed more easily, relieved that his navigation had brought them all safely three-quarters of the way around the globe, without veering seriously off course or getting lost.

Land was in sight, but the squalls were growing blacker, and the seas higher. Spray was beginning to shoot up over the bows as the vessels dipped in steeper and steeper troughs. They were making for the land, hoping to find a safe harbor, but hour by hour the wind was rising, and the sky darkening, immense black and purple clouds piling high, some streaked with coppery-orange, until an ominous gloom lay over the sea and the air grew heavy and clammy.

The crew's elation began to fade as, preparing for the coming storm, they closed the hatches and locked the sea chests, tied down the remaining panic-stricken animals and struggled to take in sail. Shut into the dark hold, Mary heard their running footsteps and felt the growing tension as the wind rose even higher and broken water roared over the bow. She felt the shock of each crashing wave, the *Charlotte* shivering, her timbers straining and creaking loudly as if in protest at the ill-treatment wrought by the storm. Thunder rolled and boomed incessantly, bringing with it the equally loud sound of torrents of rain striking the deck with great force. Every time the ship heeled over sharply as fierce gusts caught the sails, Mary and the other women shrieked in terror, imagining that she would never right herself again.

And then there was the baby, tiny Charlotte, red-faced and crying, unable to nurse or sleep. Mary did what she could to comfort her, but the wild rocking of the ship meant that comfort was not to be found, not for Charlotte, not for anyone. Wrapped in a scrap of blanket or a shred of torn canvas, or perhaps in some of Governor Phillip's burlap sacking, Charlotte cried, then whimpered, her little hands clutching at her mother, while all around her the forces of wind and rain gathered for their ultimate assault.

Hour after hour the gale lashed at the convoy in full fury, whipping the sea into immense peaks, whistling through the rigging, tearing the topsails off the *Golden Grove* and wrenching the main yard off the *Prince of Wales*. The *Charlotte* wallowed on, sometimes almost broadside to the wind, taking each of the huge combers as it came, somehow enduring the violent crashing of the waves against its wooden sides again and again. With each juddering crash,

Mary feared the timbers would give way. The relentless breakers struck like the blows of a battering ram, constant and unremitting. Surely the ship could not endure such incessant torment for long, surely the planks would splinter, then give way entirely, the white water rushing in to smother them all and drown them.

As bad as her fear and anxiety were, Mary's sickness was worse. For like all the other women she was seasick, dizzy and ill and vomiting, so sick she almost wanted the ship to stave in so that she could die. Each heave and roll of the vessel made her stomach lurch, her head burst anew with pain. It was all she could do to hold on, in her wretchedness, praying for relief from the ongoing nightmare while trying to comfort her ill baby.

The convict women "were so terrified that most of them were down on their knees at prayers," wrote Surgeon Bowes, recalling the terrible storm that struck the fleet. Retching, praying, cursing fate yet begging for deliverance, Mary spent the long day and night of January 10 and 11 waiting—waiting to die, waiting to be sick again, waiting for deliverance from the storm.

And at last, having roared and raged all night and far into the following day, the wind began to slacken slightly, the huge waves became less mountainous and the frenzy of wind and water abated to a restless heaving and churning. Exhausted, crew and convicts slept. When they awoke the wind had fallen further, the rain had finally ceased and the sun shone over rolling swells. Albatrosses, petrels and gulls swooped and dove on the air currents, and the ochre hills of Van Diemen's Land loomed on the horizon.

Dazed, thirsty, queasy, the survivors of the storm stumbled up on the deck of the *Charlotte*, hardly believing themselves alive. There it was, land, solid ground, coming closer as the onshore breeze drove the vessel forward.

Their prayers had been answered. One by one the convicts, sailors and crew lifted their weary, thin faces to the southern sun and gratefully felt its warmth. Their ceaseless journeying was nearly at an end.

VII

ANOTHER WEEK OF SAILING in clear weather brought the fleet around the southern shore of Van Diemen's Land and into Botany Bay, where on the morning of January 20, 1788, they anchored.

But when Governor Phillip and his officers went ashore, they stepped out on marshy, desolate ground, sandy in patches, devoid of the rich meadowland Captain Cook had written about in his account of his discoveries. The harbor was large, but shallow, and offered no shelter from the strong easterly winds; ships of large draught would have to anchor in the wide harbor mouth, where they would be vulnerable to gales. On shore, there was only a limited supply of fresh water.

"No place was found in the whole circuit of Botany Bay which seemed at all calculated for the reception of so large a settlement," Governor Phillip wrote in his log.[1]

So this was what it all had come to, eight months and more of battling winds and currents, storms and seasickness, deprivation and hardship: a marshy, windswept waste, completely unsuited for starting a new colony.

They could not stay in Botany Bay, or they would die.

The terrible reality sank in; the governor and his officers and lieutenants must have been dismayed in the extreme. Clearly they could not stay, but where were they to go? Captain Cook had reported on another large harbor, immediately to the north of Botany Bay, which he had named Port Jackson in honor of an admiralty judge, George Jackson.

On January 22, 1788, the fleet sailed toward the narrow harbor mouth of Botany Bay only to encounter a strong onshore wind that hampered maneuvering. The *Friendship* and the *Prince of Wales* fouled one another's lines, the *Friendship*'s jibboom crashed to the deck and she foundered, running foul of the *Charlotte*. Suddenly all the ships were in peril, unable to turn for lack of room, the helmsmen trying desperately to avoid collisions. The water was deep, the tide strong in the narrow channel that ran between jagged rocks. Sailors struggled to free the ships from one another's ropes and anchor chains before the vessels ran against the sharp rocks, with all hands in danger of being thrown into the water.

"If it had not been by the greatest good luck," wrote Clark in his journal, "we should have both [the *Friendship* and the *Charlotte*] been on shore or the rocks, and the ships must all have been lost, and the greater part, if not the whole, on board drowned, for we should have gone to pieces in less than half an hour."[2]

Somehow they managed to untangle the crossed lines, wait for a lull in the wind and let the tide carry them, one by one, out of the harbor mouth. On January 26 they stood into

Port Jackson, sailing between North and South Heads and entering the wide and beautiful bay.

So large and commodious was this long, fjordlike anchorage that Governor Phillip pronounced it "one of the finest harbors in the world, in which a thousand sail of the line might ride in perfect security."[3] For Port Jackson—modern Sydney Harbor—seemed not to be one bay but many, fringed with innumerable small and large coves, framed by jutting headlands, thickly wooded hills and a vista of stunning loveliness. The expanse of bright water shone in the sun, the wide sky stretched blue and cloudless overhead. On the shore, those on deck could make out immense rocks overhanging the summits of the hills, tall trees with silver-green leaves and among the trees, flocks of pink parrots and white cockatoos, and tiny green budgerigars, flashes of vivid color against the duller backdrop of pale verdure, tufts of dry grass and scrub.

The scent of eucalyptus was in the air, pungent and distinctive and unlike anything the travellers had encountered before. And with it, as the first of the dinghies came ashore, was another smell, the fishy smell of oysters from the mounds of white oyster shells piled on the beaches, and also whiffs of decay and putrefaction from the small corpses of bats and birds that littered the ground.

Boatload by boatland, the officers and crew, marines and male convicts began coming ashore, hauling their tools and provisions, canvas for tents and supplies of foodstuffs. Pens had to be constructed quickly for the cows and horses, poultry and greyhounds—hundreds of animals in all. Tents had to be pitched and firewood collected, and a large supply of fresh water found.

Not until leaky temporary shelters had been erected, crude huts for the officers and barracks for the marines, rows of tents for the convicts, were the women prisoners allowed to leave the transport ships and come ashore, on February 6, 1788.

Mary stepped out onto the hot sandy beach Governor Phillip had named Sydney Cove, blinking in the glare of the strong sunlight, gaunt and pale from her many months in the ship's hold. She was rail-thin, and she stumbled uncertainly as she took her first steps onto the hot sand, for her legs, long accustomed to the heave and roll of the ship, could not at first adjust to the unvarying horizontal of solid ground.

The sand burned her feet, shod as they were in the sad remnants of her shoes, which left her nearly barefoot. Her shabby, salt-stained, much-mended gown—the best she had, most likely the only one she had—showed the ill effects of constant soaking in seawater and stank of the bilge; it was badly in need of washing and drying in the sun. She could not help looking bedraggled, and may well have had the hollow-eyed, sallow-faced look of one who has been ill, for many of the convicts who came off the ships in that February of 1788 were still suffering from scurvy and dysentery, and all were malnourished. Even Commander Phillip was suffering from a severe pain in his side.[4]

Holding baby Charlotte in the crook of one arm, Mary used the other to fan away the flies that assaulted her eyes, nose and mouth in dozens, trying to crawl into her nostrils and down her throat. She had grown used to insect tormentors—the nits that lodged in her long unkempt brown hair, the lice that had infested her skin ever since her stay in Exeter jail, if not before—but in Port Jackson Mary was to encounter a new set of pests, of which the flies were only the harbingers.[5]

With the other convict women Mary and Charlotte sheltered from the heat of the day in the temporary tent assigned to her, in the area set aside for the women's use. She could hardly rest, there was so much noise and excitement all around, the tramp of boots and the rattle of chains, the sounds of hammering and sawing, of men shouting to one another as they worked, of trees being felled and dragged past the sprawl of tents, the crying of children and the squalling of chickens and geese and the bellowing of cattle. Marines mustered to the rattle of drums. And on the beach, sailors shouted and swore as they unloaded the dinghies that came and went all day from the transports, loaded with chests and boxes, barrels and baskets.

Amid all the hubbub there was an undercurrent of sheer animal arousal, for the coming ashore of the women meant that for the first time, the sexes could be together without the impediments of wooden walls or gratings. There had been much coupling aboard the ships, mainly between the convict women and the sailors and marines; many babies had been born—including Mary's baby Charlotte—and no doubt much jealousy had been aroused, and quarrels had arisen. Now, however, all these erotic crosscurrents could be played out on the wide stage of the new settlement, and hardly had dusk fallen over Port Jackson on the evening of February 6 when there began a prolonged and exuberant release of pent-up lust.

They coupled in tents, in the woods, on the beach, anywhere they found one another. It was as if a temporary madness had descended, the familiar madness of sailors come ashore, eager to carouse and celebrate and itching to copulate. Many of the women were as eager as the men, though some, like the convict Elizabeth Needham, fled her marine lover who beat her "because she would not go up into the woods with him." Others of the women, ambushed by men as the women came from bathing, were raped and had to be rescued.[6]

As if in counterpoint to the storm of sexual revelry and predation, the heavens opened and the settlement was drenched in a hard-driving rain. Now couples grappled in the mud, under upturned dinghies, under improvised shelters, while the wind tore at their clothing and sent leaves whirling over the hard ground and into their faces.

It was a tempestuous night, the men and women alike drunk on what one of them called the "vile Rio spirits" brought from Brazil, "so offensive both in taste and smell that he must be fond of drinking indeed that can use it." Some were so drunk they collapsed in a haze of boozy contentment, but others went reeling and belching through the camp in search of partners, swearing and belligerent. In the interims between lovemaking and rapine, fights broke out; heads were broken, faces scratched and bleeding. Jilted lovers took vengeance, rivals confronted one another with bloody consequences.

Some of the evangelicals and other churchgoers among the crew and marines looked on the freewheeling saturnalia and pronounced it depraved.

"It is beyond my abilities to give a just description of the scene of debauchery and riot that ensued during the night," wrote Arthur Bowes, assistant surgeon on the *Lady Penrhyn*. "The anarchy and confusion which reigns and the audacity of the convicts, both men and women, is arrived to such a pitch as is not to be equalled by any other set of villains on the globe," was Lieutenant Ralph Clark's judgment.[7]

But if some were shocked and judgmental, Governor Phillip looked on the carousals—and even, at first, the criminal behavior—with a lenient eye. He was accustomed to the shoreward exuberance of sailors; some excesses were to be expected. And had not the women been brought to Port Jackson expressly to provide a sexual outlet for the men? It was their primary function. Only, he noted, there were not enough women—nearly four men to every woman. He would have to send to England for more female convicts.[8]

Opportunists that many of them were, it did not take the women long to realize that, there being far fewer of them than there were of the men, they could market themselves profitably. Many of them had been prostitutes in England, now they would be prostitutes in Port Jackson. The women's camp was nicknamed "Sodom," the "whores' camp," and despite efforts to police it, Ralph Clark thought that "there is more sin committed in it than in any other part of the world."[9] "Sodom" was raided periodically, and the unfortunate sailors and crew members who were found there were bound and force-marched out of the camp, in hopes that the disgrace would prevent them from returning.[10]

Many of Mary's fellow convicts chose to barter their bodies for money or food or whatever else they could command. But Mary, for reasons that can only be conjectured, chose marriage instead.

It may be that Mary was pregnant with her future husband's child, and wanted a father for the new baby as well as for Charlotte. Or perhaps she simply wanted to escape the increasing rowdiness of the camp, and the risk of rape or other injury. She may well have been raped already, on board the *Charlotte* and/or the *Dunkirk*; under what circumstances her daughter was conceived is unknown. She may, in choosing to marry, have wanted to acquire a protector, for the unruliness in the camp was growing worse by the day; convict men were whipped for fighting, and flogged for assaulting women, while convict women were given twenty-five to thirty lashes for brawling and creating a disturbance. Sodom was little more than a brothel, with the men coming and going at all hours and violent quarrels erupting frequently.

Mary may have been pressured by others to join in the pros- titution, or persecuted if she did not. Every night, to the accompaniment of recurring lightning storms, there were drunken trysts, sordid sexual transactions—and, one hopes, some tender exchanges between cherished lovers.

Just how and when Mary agreed to marry William Bryant, the Cornish smuggler whom she had known on the *Charlotte* as the dispenser of rations, cannot now be discov- ered. Possibly they agreed to marry while still on shipboard. Or perhaps Will proposed to Mary amid the bustle and erotic ferment of the settlement's first few days. It may have been a union of convenience, for the governor offered to give plots of land to those convicts who married, and Mary and Will Bryant saw the value of that offer and decided to take advantage of it.

One thing is clear, however. In becoming Mary Broad's husband, Will Bryant did not believe that he was entering into a legal marriage, or that his obligations to his wife would extend beyond his term of sentence in Australia. What Mary's view of the legality of her marriage was, no contemporary document records.

Will made his opinion known to others, saying "that he did not consider his marriage in this country as binding," and expressing the widely held sentiment among the convicts that once his sentence expired, in 1791, he would be free to leave Port Jackson—and his wife.[11]

Of course, Will Bryant may have been married already. Many of the male convicts who took wives in the new set- tlement had left wives and families behind in England.[12] Bigamy was to become commonplace in the new colony. And it is conceivable that Mary too was married—and that she shared William's view that whatever vows she took in Port Jackson would only be provisional, not permanent.

With whatever degree of devotion, opportunism or cynicism they felt, Mary Broad and William Bryant stood before the chaplain, Reverend Richard Johnson, on February 10, 1788, and repeated their marriage vows. The service was in the open air, held "under a great tree," and there were four other couples married at the same time, along with three christenings. Will Bryant signed the marriage register "in a legible hand," but Mary could only mark it with an X.

No doubt there were toasts to the newlyweds after the service, drunk in vile Rio spirits, and bawdy jokes, and good wishes from the governor (who had admonished the convicts that they ought to marry, "assuring them that an indiscriminate and illegal intercourse would be punished with the greatest severity and rigor") and from the couples' friends.[13] Catherine Fryer, Mary's companion in crime, may have been in attendance, with her infant, and Surgeon White and the officers from the *Charlotte.*

Mary and Will spent their wedding night in their unfinished hut at the inlet the colonists had named Farm Cove, removed from the tent city and its noise and confusions. They belonged to each other, at least for the time being. They would make a home, work together, nurture Charlotte, and bring other children into the world. Perhaps they loved each other, or would learn to; perhaps not. But as Mary lay down beside her husband that night, and listened to the unfamiliar twitterings and scratching noises of the animals outside, she knew that she had done well for herself. She had left Sodom behind, and cast her lot with a hardworking, clever man who was bound to do well for himself, and for the three of them, in the uncertain future.

VIII

*T*HE FIRST FLEET had arrived in Port Jackson in January of 1788; by April it was evident that despite the beauty of its setting and the promise of its climate, the land was sterile, its climate impossible, and its apparently abundant resources a delusion.

Nothing would grow in the carefully cleared and painstakingly planted fields. Vines flourished, but the seeds brought from England for growing grain and flax (which was to have been the new colony's chief crop), and the coffee and indigo plants, and the cotton and cochineal fig cuttings brought from Rio, failed to germinate or take root. Weevils destroyed the wheat and barley. There was not enough fresh water, and what water there was, gave the colonists worms and dysentery.[1] Foodstores, kept under "wretched covers of thatch," rotted in the rain and were at risk of fire from the nightly lightning storms.[2] Fresh food spoiled rapidly in the extreme heat. The convicts learned to eat snakes ("palatable and nutritive," but difficult to stew), kangaroo meat (which they devoured "with avidity," considering the tail the choicest part) and fish, plus the old salt meat from the ships' stores and the local green plant they called "scurvy grass" in an effort to prevent the worst disease scourge they had yet encountered.

The weather, which was a constant preoccupation, varied from sweltering heat to chill. On the hottest days, the sun bore down with great force from early morning on, the temperature rising in midafternoon to 110 degrees or higher. The air felt "like the blast of a heated oven," and the colonists took shelter in their flimsy huts and tents. Plants shrivelled and died, convicts fainted from sunstroke and parakeets died in midair and dropped lifeless to the ground. Fruit bats, which lived in the trees, succumbed to the terrible heat and also fell to the ground in great numbers. But every few days it was necessary to light fires in the evening, so cold was the air, and often easterly winds brought clouds and storms, hailstones and hard rain.

It was not long before harsh weather and contaminated water, exposure and malnutrition spread disease through the settlement. Scurvy reappeared, convicts, marines and sailors came to the new hospital complaining of swollen gums, fever or pains in the legs and chest. Surgeon White knew that eating vegetables would alleviate the symptoms, but there were no vegetables, only scurvy grass, and so the numbers of patients with the disorder "rose to a most alarming height," as the surgeon noted in his journal, and the most serious cases began to die.

An area had been designated as a cemetery, an empty plot of ground at the end of a row of partially completed buildings including the church, storehouses and hospital.

Graves were dug for the victims of scurvy, alongside the small, shallow graves for nine of the infants born in the early months of the colony that did not survive and the deeper, larger graves for the two male convicts who were murdered and the two more, one very young, one old, who were executed for theft.

Altogether, by one reckoning, there were at least fifty-seven graves in the waste ground next to the hospital, and in the first six months at Port Jackson, many more people died than were born.[3] One of the convicts, a woman of eighty-two, hanged herself. Several more of the convicts were killed by falling trees, and one man died after eating a poisonous wild plant. There were hazards enough—Port Jackson was infested with venomous black snakes and tiger snakes, and there were large sharks in the bay. Venereal disease spread rapidly. Governor Phillip pronounced it a "severe scourge," and doubted whether it could ever be eradicated. And as the season advanced toward winter, people began to die from cholera and dysentery, and more funerals were held several times a week.

Mary, now Mrs. William Bryant, shared the common vicissitudes of her fellow convicts in the antipodean summer and fall of 1788 without succumbing to their worst dangers. With the others, she and Will attended the executions—held at sunset, the full complement of marines under arms—and watched as those convicted, old and young, were summarily dispatched. One, an "old and desperate offender," died with a "hardy spirit," wrote Watkin Tench, a marine officer who kept a detailed journal of the early days of the new settlement. The others may have been pitiable.[4]

In marrying Will, Mary had managed to avoid living in the squalor of Sodom, while enjoying the advantages her husband had: prestige, status, uncommon comforts, even servants of sorts.

For Will Bryant was a person of consequence in Port Jackson, as he had been aboard the *Charlotte*. Just as he had been entrusted, on shipboard, with the vital task of measuring out the food rations to the other convicts, so in Port Jackson he was entrusted with organizing the critical task of catching fish for the settlement.

"From his having been bred from his youth to the business of a fisherman in the Western part of England," wrote the Judge Advocate David Collins in his *Account of the English Colony in New South Wales,* "William Bryant was given the management and direction of such boats as were employed in fishing."[5] Knowing that the temptation to hoard the catch or barter some of the fish on the side would be great, the governor did his best to forestall this potential breach of trust. Not only was a hut built for Will and Mary, but according to Collins "he wanted for nothing that was necessary or that was suitable to a person of his description and situation." Most important, Will was allowed to keep some of his catch—an inducement to catch as much fish as possible, so that his share would be substantial.

Other than that he was twenty-five or twenty-six years old in 1788, that he was a Cornishman, perhaps from Launceston, and that despite having been accused of smuggling and convicted of forgery he impressed some higher-ups as a man of good and honest character (others were dubious), little is known of Will Bryant.[6] He had the daring—or the desperation—to resist the Revenue officers when they tried to seize some stolen goods he had. He had sufficient physical stamina and vitality to survive the harrowing conditions of the First Fleet voyage. And he married a strong-willed fellow survivor of the voyage—though whether marriage would, in the long run, prove to be an advantage or not was yet to be determined.

In 1788 Will was four years into his seven-year sentence. In three years he would be a free man. All he had to do was be patient, supply the colony with fish, and wait. Before he was thirty he would have served his sentence.[7]

Some of the convicts who were married in the early weeks of the settlement repented of their rash acts and tried to have their marriages annulled. They had only married because of the comforts and privileges married couples were offered, chiefly better housing and plots of land. But being disappointed in their expectations, they had second thoughts.[8] The marriages were not dissolved.

"Everyone is so taken up with their miseries that they have no pity to bestow on others," wrote one female convict that first autumn in Port Jackson. To the deprivations of too little food and inadequate shelter and the perils of illness and enervation from overwork was the added distress caused by nightly thefts. Tobacco, liquor, clothing, whatever was in short supply—chiefly food—was pilfered, and the marines did not seem able to prevent the epidemic of crimes. In fact, the marines were among the worst offenders, brawling and carousing, quarreling noisily in the early hours of the morning, ultimately even complicit in causing grievous injury to one of their number.[9] Having gotten a duplicate key to the public storehouses, the soldiers snuck inside, taking meat and flour and spirits, and hiding them in the huts of their accomplices in Sodom. Over a period of months, taking small amounts each time, the marines stole a large quantity of foodstuffs and other goods, until they were caught, "by accident," and tried and executed.[10]

If the marines were criminous and subversive of order, their commander, the settlement's vice-governor, Major Robert Ross, was even worse. To the convicts, he was the scourge of the colony. For Ross was more than a disciplinarian, he was a persecutor, universally hated for his severe punishments. An embittered, hostile personality, to judge from contemporary accounts, Ross despised the convicts, his own marines, and in particular his staff. It was Ross, and not the relatively milder Governor Phillip, who ordered the floggings—twenty lashes, forty lashes, seventy-five lashes at a time—and who summoned the entire population of Port Jackson, upwards of nine hundred people, to watch as the savage punishments were administered.

Three heavy wooden posts were joined to form a triangle. Then the victim was tied to the posts by his upraised wrists, his legs spread apart. While a detachment of marines stood by, the drummer beating out a tattoo, a beefy marine with a strong arm delivered the blows with a cat-o'-nine-tails, which lacerated the flesh unmercifully.

The first few blows left the victim's back in shreds; by the time twenty-five lashes had been delivered the poor screaming wretch had fainted from the pain, his back laid open and quivering involuntarily and his blood flowing freely from a hundred open wounds. The officers' greyhounds licked eagerly at the blood, birds pecked at the chunks of bloody flesh that flew in all directions with each brutal stroke. By the time the full complement of blows had been given, and the injured man dragged off, the ground beneath the triangle was crimson and sodden, and the witnesses, sobered by what they had seen, drifted back to their occupations, cursing Major Ross and dreading what future punishments might come to each of them.

June 4, 1788, came, the king's birthday, and to mark the occasion the *Sirius* and the *Supply* fired twenty-one-gun salutes at dawn, one o'clock in the afternoon, and sunset. From shore, the marine battalion fired three volleys with their muskets at noon, and sent up three cheers for George III.

It was a red-letter day, the first day since the fleet landed five months earlier that no one went to bed hungry. The convicts were given extra rations, and an allowance of grog. At night they celebrated around bonfires—shivering in the cold, for winter had settled in—and rejoiced in the knowledge that the governor had given them three days' holiday.[11] Four convicts who were suffering under sentence of banishment and had been languishing on an island in the bay, were loosed from their fetters and pardoned, and for a few brief hours, with everyone replete and happily mellow, the mood of the settlement lightened and private griefs and miseries were temporarily laid aside.

The marine officers and principal officials of the colony went to the governor's house to dine on mutton, pork, wild duck, fish, pies and preserved fruits and kangaroo tail. They toasted the king with port Madeira, sherry and porter, offering toast after toast to His Majesty, and Sydney Cove, and the Prince of Wales, the queen and royal family, the king's brother the Duke of Cumberland, the king's ministers and minions.

"Prosperity to Sydney Cove!" a voice shouted, and all present expressed fervent assent and drank to the colony's wealth, while the marine band played "God Save the King" and several rousing marches.

Governor Phillip, in evident pain, probably from a kidney stone, presided as graciously as his severe pangs would allow, and announced to the assembled company that he had decided to name their settlement Albion.[12] With his guests he walked out into the chilly evening to watch the bonfires, and returned some time later to offer them a late evening meal. The day ended, Surgeon White wrote, in "pleasantry, good humor and cheerfulness," and the mood lingered into the following day, only to be dampened by the discovery that a number of thefts had been committed during the night.[13]

No one in the colony knew that in distant London, at the royal court, His Majesty George III was desperately unwell with a mysterious nervous disease and that within months he would be strapped into a straitjacket and pronounced unfit to reign. The welfare of Port Jackson, his new antipodean settlement, was as far as possible from his disordered thoughts.

IX

*E*SCAPE! It was on the minds of all the convicts, sleeping and waking. They planned and schemed, separately and together, most of them certain, in his or her most optimistic moments, that the day of liberation would soon be at hand.

Within days of the First Fleet's arrival in Port Jackson a number of convicts managed to get away and return to Botany Bay, where two French ships chartered by the explorer Jean-François de La Pérouse were on a brief sojourn in the harbor. The escapees begged La Pérouse to take them aboard. He refused, and in the first week of February, 1788, all but two of the half-starved convicts returned to Port Jackson to face their inevitable punishment.[1] It was generally assumed that the two who did not return, Ann Smith and Peter Paris, had managed to get away somehow, probably on the French ships.[2] Four convict women took off into the woods, intent on escape. The sailors shot at them, and three of them were recaptured, but the fourth, like Ann Smith, was presumed to have gotten away.

An imaginative convict named Daly, "a notorious thief and impostor," according to Tench, concocted a plan to lure a party of marines into the wilderness, intending to go with them and then, when an opportunity arose, leave them behind and seize his freedom. Daly took a pair of metal buckles, pounded them into fragments, mixed the glittering metal fragments with sand and small stones, and then announced that he had found a gold mine. The prepared earth, he said, had come from the mine and the shards of metal were pure gold.

Few announcements could have caused greater excitement. A search party was quickly selected, and set off, following Daly, into the unknown interior. For days the searchers, with Daly in the lead, wandered through expanses of gum trees and across open plains toward the distant mountains. But in the end the search proving fruitless, and Daly, finding no opportunity to escape, eventually confessed to the hoax and took his punishment. But he inspired others to concoct similar schemes. Nearly every day, Tench wrote, convicts came forward with stories of "large, fresh water rivers, valuable ores, and quarries of limestone, chalk, and marble."[3] There was no end to the prisoners' inventiveness, or to their ingenuity. Each extravagant claim had to be pursued, in case it proved to be true. And each search party that left the settlement provided yet another opportunity for one more convict to escape.

In June of 1788, around the time of the celebration for George III's birthday, a convict named Edward Corbett took off into the brush after he stole a woman's gown. He was gone for weeks. The others presumed that he had either died or found his way to a new life. Then one day Corbett returned, hollow-eyed and grotesquely thin, with barely enough energy left to stumble into the camp and identify himself. He had been in the wilderness for three weeks, with little to eat, fearful and terribly cold—it snowed that winter—and frightened almost to death by two things he had experienced.

The first was a strong earthquake, which all the colonists felt along with Corbett, and which many of them interpreted as an omen of disaster.

The second was seeing a severed head, the head of a fellow convict, lying near the remains of a bonfire. Discernible in the ashes of the bonfire was a decapitated corpse.[4]

Corbett was in no doubt about the identity of the severed head. It belonged to a man kidnapped by the aboriginals—"the natives," as the colonists called them—and subsequently murdered. During his weeks away from Port Jackson Corbett had spent quite a bit of time with members of the Iora tribe, but found that they did not like his company and shunned him. They were never menacing, merely unwelcoming. But when Corbett saw the remains of his fellow convict, he realized that he might be murdered himself. So he fled—not deeper into the unknown interior, but back to Port Jackson.

The Ioras (for it was members of this tribe, rather than the nearby Daruks and Tarawal, that the First Fleet settlers most often encountered) were a constant presence in the background of the Europeans' lives from the moment they sailed into Botany Bay. Fishing in their canoes, shelling oysters beside the shore, roasting fish and meat over open cooking fires, standing singly or in small groups around the shoreline or walking through the stands of trees, the Australian aborigines were there in their hundreds, part of the landscape.

From the Europeans' point of view, the Ioras lived so simply, and were so lacking in the rudiments of civilized life, as to be all but bestial; the educated few among the colonists, such as Surgeon White, were familiar with Rousseau's idealization of men and women living in the state of nature, but these tribal groupings seemed too primal in their living arrangements to fit Rousseau's parameters.

They wore no clothes and never bathed, they smeared their bodies with fish oil to keep the mosquitoes away and hence acquired, over the course of their lives, a thick patina of earth, filth, and human and animal ordure. They were very skillful in throwing their long spears and wielding their long wooden swords and immense clubs, but lacked the craft of building houses or indeed any structures, could not make pots or fashion articles from metal, and were even ignorant of the bow and arrow.[5] They roamed with their fellow tribesmen but did not settle anywhere for long, did not plant crops, shared everything in common and were apparently leaderless. All of the arts of civilized life, as the Europeans understood civilization, were beyond the Ioras' ken.

To Mary, who knew nothing of Rousseau or of the idea of the noble savage, the Ioras must have seemed, as they did to Tench, "hideous" and frightening. Naked, dark men (very few women were glimpsed), "deep chocolate" in color, their bodies adorned with the scars of self-inflicted wounds, their noses pierced with fish bones: all this must have seemed monstrous, especially when they painted themselves red or white with pipe clay. Nothing had prepared Mary for the alarming encounters she and the other convicts had with the aboriginals, who helped themselves to fish from the convicts' and marines' nets and attempted to annoy the newcomers by setting fire to their "combustible matter" with their firesticks.[6] They stared rudely, and chattered to one another in a language of which only one word, *"Wurra!"* ("Go away!") was intelligible to the Europeans because of the dismissive and threatening gestures they made when they shouted it.

Whenever she left her hut in Farm Cove, Mary had to be watchful for the half-wild dingo dogs the Ioras kept, especially when she had her infant daughter Charlotte with her. The dingos disliked the Europeans, so the Ioras, Tench wrote, were "sometimes mischievous enough to set them on single persons whom they chance to meet in the woods." The dogs worried the convicts and marines and gnawed at their ankles. Occasionally one of the officers, attempting to shoot birds with his fowling piece, or one of the convicts designated by Governor Phillip to hunt kangaroos, would be set upon by a dingo and would shoot it.[7]

Fear of the Ioras escalated after Edward Corbett's story of the severed head was repeated throughout the settlement. Tension had already escalated, for only a month before Corbett's return to Port Jackson, two convicts who had been cutting rushes at some distance from Sydney Cove were butchered by tribal spears and clubs. One was skewered in the belly, the other was bludgeoned to death, his skull crushed. This gory attack followed close on another, in which a convict was speared in the hip and another abducted.[8]

A dozen convicts had disappeared since the fleet landed in January, including Ann Smith and the other female escapee. Now the convicts began to wonder, and to ask one another when they met to talk of escape, whether none of their number had actually made it to safety. Had all of them been speared, or fatally wounded, or taken captive by the Ioras? Was there, in fact, no safe escape possible by land?

Tench detected a "spirit of rapine and intrusion" among the tribesmen—provoked, no doubt, by the convicts' aggression toward them. The convicts stole the Ioras' canoes and spears and—despite Governor Phillip's stern warnings against any sort of violence against the "natives"—attacked them from time to time.[9] Relations worsened during the winter and spring of 1788, with three more prisoners wounded and one killed. The aggravating, and very dangerous, fires continued to be set. And when, one day, a marine officer and two companions suddenly came upon what appeared to be a war party of fourteen Ioras walking behind their painted war leader, each carrying a spear and a large stone, the three Europeans froze in sudden alarm.

As it turned out, they need not have worried. The tribesmen passed on, hardly taking note of the three men from Port Jackson—just as the three hundred or so tribesmen the governor had glimpsed on one of his exploratory journeys ignored him and his companions, intent as they were on their own pursuits.[10]

Still, incidents of harm continued, and added to the growing atmosphere of worry and fear, and the constant talk of escape.

Winter in Port Jackson proved to be as severely cold as summer had been severely hot. Hoarfrost rimed the unfinished huts and storehouses, and a shallow crust of ice particles formed at the edges of small ponds. One storm after another blew up the harbor, rain swirling along the inlets and drenching the settlement. The thermometer was at the freezing point, and some snow fell.[11] Squalls brought violent thunderstorms, the water in the bay grew very cold and when Will Bryant went out to fish, his catches became smaller and smaller. The turtles the convicts had once caught on Lord Howe Island—a small island some five hundred miles east of Port Jackson—were no longer to be found there, and for the first time the governor and his officers had to confront the possibility that without substantial supplies from England or elsewhere the entire population of Port Jackson would very likely starve.

Each member of the colony was given his or her ration of eight pounds of flour a week, along with five pounds of maggoty salt pork, three pints of peas and six ounces of butter. But the butter was rancid and the flour moldy with age; the salt pork was barely edible and the peas far from fresh. Fish, in increasingly small amounts, was what the convicts, marines and seamen survived on—supplemented by snakes and lizards, fern roots that they dug in the swamp, berries they had found in the woods in summer and pre-served ("destitute of flavor and nutrition," Tench thought), and oysters and scurvy grass, washed down with tea brewed from a plant with a sweetish flavor that they called "sweet tea."[12]

All the cattle had run off, the bulls and cows being much more successful at escaping than the prisoners. There were still hogs and poultry in the pens, but all but one of the sheep brought from Cape Town had died, some of them elec-trocuted by lightning. Fresh provisions of any sort had become "scarcer than in a blockaded town," Tench wrote, and it was only through luck and the saving hand of provi-dence that starvation was forestalled.

"Had it not been for a stray kangaroo, which fortune now and then threw our way, we should have been utter strangers to the taste of fresh food."[13] Kangaroo meat was indeed welcome, but it was lean, it did not restore the thin colonists to plumpness. Only bread and milk and suet and gravy, and plenty of them, could do that. So in October of 1788, Governor Phillip sent the *Sirius* to Cape Town for supplies, and the entire colony waited, poised between hope and dread as the months passed, for her return.

A month after the departure of the *Sirius*, only the little storeship *Supply* was left in the vast harbor. The last of the transports departed, bound for new destinations, and the community at Sydney Cove was cut off from the outside world. It had been nearly a year since the fleet weighed anchor, the hot weather had returned and with it, the scorching days and thunderstorms of summer. Far from flourishing in the new land, the colonists were much worse off than they had been when they landed. To their list of hardships was now added the psychological hardship of having to overcome their fears, and their newfound sense of isolation.

But even as desolation threatened to overwhelm the colonists, their innate desire to survive intervened. The toughest and most determined of them did what they had to to keep themselves alive: they resorted to pilfering.

Plants grown in the communal gardens and in the kitchen gardens of private huts were stolen and eaten before they matured. Storehouses were broken into and raided. Attempts were made to steal food from the Ioras—who seemed, in the midst of what appeared to the Europeans barren land, to have plenty to eat. And Will and Mary Bryant, through whose hands passed the principal food of the colony, had for a long time been secretly keeping a larger portion of that food for themselves and baby Charlotte.

Will had been dishonest in reporting his catch from the day he was made principal fisherman for the colony. He and Mary always kept something extra—beyond what they were officially allowed to keep from the catch—and secretly traded the fish with other convicts for liquor, clothing or other goods. Will was a smuggler, practiced in secret trading and habituated, as all the convicts were, to outlawry; though

he may have been able to give the appearance of honest deal-
ing, he was fundamentally dishonest, a black marketeer on a
small scale.

Mary came from a community where smuggling and a
black market in smuggled goods flourished. It would
have been against Mary and Will's nature not to take
advantage of the position of trust Will enjoyed as principal
fisherman.[14]

Certainly by late 1788 the Bryants were keeping back
significant quantities of sole, skate and mullet, bass and
grouper from the ever dwindling catch and selling or trading
them. Their ally in this increasingly flourishing illegal activity was another convict, Joseph Paget, who had known Mary
on the hulk *Dunkirk* and had sailed with Mary and Will on
the *Charlotte*. Paget may have been a Cornishman like the
Bryants; he was convicted at Exeter assizes, and had some
skill as a fisherman himself.[15] He fished with Will, and was
also a house servant of sorts to the Bryants.

But something went wrong. Possibly Paget became jeal-
ous, or a personal quarrel broke out, or Paget demanded a
greater share in the rewards of the illegal trade, tried to
blackmail the Bryants, and was unsuccessful. Whatever his
motivation, in February of 1789 Paget went to Judge
Advocate Collins and revealed what had been going on.

Will had to be tried for his crime, there was no alternative. Valuable, even essential, he might be to the colony, but
theft of food was a very grave offense, a hanging offense. The
judge advocate had to try him.

Will was seized and shackled and put under guard. A
court was hastily set up, and Paget gave his evidence.
Surgeon White spoke up for Will, saying he had never been
other than "strictly honest" when serving as provisioner
aboard the *Charlotte*. But the surgeon could not vouch for

what had or had not gone on in Port Jackson. And besides, the temptation now was far greater than it had ever been aboard ship, and the need for food more acute. No one else seems to have spoken up for Will.

He was convicted, but not, after all, hanged. Instead he was sentenced to receive a hundred lashes and stripped of his post as principal fisherman, deprived of his hut in Farm Cove and reduced to the status of a disgraced, twice-convicted felon, to be held in contempt for having betrayed the entire colony and put its survival in peril.

The entire population of Sydney Cove was ordered to assemble to witness the protracted flogging of William Bryant. The marines took up their positions alongside the flogging triangle. Drums beat, the prisoner was brought out, and his hands tied to the top of the triangle. Stroke by cruel stroke the lash was laid to his back, while his blood ran down and gouts of flesh were torn from his body. His groans and screams were terrible.

Mary, forced to watch and listen along with Charlotte, must have burned to avenge herself and Will on their betrayer Joseph Paget, who was also in the watching crowd. Paget too was guilty—as she herself was—for both had been complicit in the stealing of the fish. But Paget had not been punished, and would not be, except for the punishing censure of his fellow convicts who abhorred betrayers. Paget had perhaps been rewarded by the governor or the judge advocate, while Will, who was so much more capable, was broken in rank and now in body. Because of Paget, Mary and Charlotte no longer had a hut to live in, or a garden to farm, but were forced to find what crude and uncomfortable shelter they could.

Thoughts of revenge must have preoccupied Mary as she stood for an hour or more under the merciless white sunlight of midday, suffering as sweat ran down her face, her breast, her arms. Will, his tender swollen back churned to red pulp by the cat-o'-nine-tails, had fainted, but still the lashing went on, methodical and thorough. At last he was freed from the triangle, senseless and bleeding.

Salt was poured into his wounds and he was dragged off to the hospital, where Surgeon White, who had done his best to defend Will, was now helpless to heal him. If his terrible wounds did not become infected, and if he did not die of fever, then in time he might be restored to himself—or a permanently crippled version of himself. But flogging victims frequently died of their trauma; there was no guarantee that Will would pull through.

Hungry and angry, Mary Bryant slept badly that hot February night, her mind on food, on revenge—and above all, on escape.

X

THE IORAS BEGAN DYING in droves in April, and by May there were bodies floating in all the coves of the harbor, hundreds of naked thin brown bodies, covered in boils and scabs, giving off an extremely offensive odor—not just the stench of decay, but the distinctive stink of smallpox.

All the colony's doctors knew the odor, and the signs of the disease, for they had encountered it many times in England, where smallpox was common, acutely painful and unresponsive to any known medical treatment. The doctors had seen many sufferers die, and were well aware that those who survived were marked for life with pitted skin and blemishes. The trauma of pain and fear left their interior marks on survivors as well, though these were harder to detect.[1] Now the scourge had been introduced to the continent of New Holland, with terrible results.

Some of the corpses were brought up out of the water and taken to the hospital, where the diagnosis was confirmed. Amazingly, despite the high risk of infection, no cases of smallpox were reported among the Europeans, though they had carried the disease, or at least a weak strain of it, and infected the aboriginal people.

To the Ioras and other aboriginal tribes, the impact of smallpox, along with cholera and influenza, was unimaginably devastating. Perhaps half their number were annihilated. To the colonists, the singular nature of the epidemic must have seemed a divine dispensation, with the Ioras and other tribes being devastated while they themselves were spared. Another evidence of divine favor—or sheer luck— came on May 2, 1789—at the peak of the fearsome smallpox epidemic—when the *Sirius* sailed into the harbor just at sunset and her guns boomed out an exuberant greeting.

Oh, the rejoicing that met the news that the warship had returned! "Universal joy and congratulation" spread from one end of Sydney Cove to the other, and out to Farm Cove and all the adjacent inlets. Now there would be fresh meat, and salt, and flour to make bread, and sugar, and fresh greens—all the things the convicts and their guardians had been missing. The list of things they needed was long: seeds, animals, farm implements, clothing, shoes, ammunition, blankets, wines and spirits, tobacco, coffee, tea, rice, thermometers to replace the six Surgeon White had broken (the last of them having been smashed on coming ashore), newspapers, books, perhaps a string or two for Surgeon Worgan's piano.

The *Sirius* had been through an ordeal. Her crew told of encountering huge expanses of ice on her thirteen-week-long eastward journey to Cape Town via Cape Horn. Even in mid-December, high summer in the southern latitudes, it had been so cold that the drinking water froze in its casks, and the crew could hardly reef the sails, their fingers were so stiff.[2] Then with the ship fully loaded, and near the end of its long return journey, rounding Tasman's Head it was almost wrecked in Storm Bay.

Each barrel, trunk and cask, as it was offloaded from the *Sirius* and brought ashore, seemed all the more precious to the colonists for having been brought so many thousands of miles at such peril. Mindful of the dangers averted, and inordinately grateful for the sudden abundance, the colonists greedily filled their bellies and warmed themselves in their new clothes against the wintry chill, forgetting their hardship and fears, their recent hunger pangs and even the dead and dying tribesmen whose diseased bodies lay on nearby shores. They feasted, were replete, and slept soundly.

In this season of abundance and renewed hope for the future, Mary Bryant became pregnant once again.

Charlotte was now twenty-one months old, having spent most of her life in New Holland. When the new baby arrived Charlotte would be two and a half, and Mary would be sure to have her hands full looking after them both. And for Will, there would be a family of four for whom he would be responsible.

Will, having eventually recovered from his severe lashing, continued to fish but under strict supervision, so that he was given no opportunity to keep back any of the catch. He did what was required of him, and presumably he lived with his pregnant wife and stepdaughter in a hut he managed to build. In outward appearance, they were a family. But Will was, at best, ambivalent about his responsibilities. With the new baby on the way, he was overheard to reiterate, when with his friends, that he did not look on his marriage as legal, because it had been solemnized in Sydney Cove and not in England.

Will's opinions carried weight, despite his conviction for theft and his demotion. Governor Phillip decided that further restrictions had to be placed on convicts who had married in the colony.

"It having been reported to the governor," the judge advocate wrote, "that Bryant had been frequently heard to say that he did not consider his marriage in this country as binding, his Excellency caused the convicts to be informed that none would be permitted to quit the country who had wives and children incapable of maintaining themselves and likely to become burdensome to the settlement."[3]

The new regulation came as a blow to all the newly married convicts—except those few with life sentences. Every convict counted the days until his or her sentence expired, for on expiration each one expected to be able to leave the settlement, provided he or she could get a berth on a ship or find some other means of returning to England. Will's sentence was due to expire in two years.[4] Now, thanks to the governor's order, he would not be able to leave until Charlotte, Mary and the new baby were no longer a burden to the settlement.

It would be many years before his dependants were able to fend for themselves, if they ever were. Mary was hardy, and had survived much; she could probably be counted on to be independent. But Charlotte and the new baby would have to be provided for for years—until Will was on the threshold of old age, and perhaps beyond.

If he heeded the governor's new order, Will was trapped. He would have to remain in Sydney Cove virtually for life.

Now he was triply aggrieved: for his convict status, for his recent trial, punishment, and demotion, and for being held in the new colony against his will past the term of his sentence. And all because he had married Mary, instead of living with her outside of marriage, as most of the convict couples did, or simply maintaining an informal liaison with her.

Did he blame Mary for his plight? Did he love her, and she him? On these vital mysteries, the contemporary records are silent. But the Bryants remained together as a family, and Mary's pregnancy went on without incident, as spring came and the settlement entered a new and more lawless phase of its collective life.

Cliques were forming, antagonisms erupting in the latter half of 1789. Surgeon White and his young Third Assistant William Balmain were so seriously at odds that they fought a duel, and both were wounded. Dishonest marines and the most rebelliously inclined of the female convicts joined forces in thieving and debauchery, the men bringing their plunder to the women's huts each night and making drunken plans for more thefts.[5] Drunkenness, always "the prevailing vice of the colony," became even more pervasive, with gambling hardly less so. The convicts gambled away their rations, their clothing, their few possessions playing dice and cards and pitch and toss. Prostitution continued to flourish, and there was even an ugly incident of child rape when one Private Henry Wright assaulted an eight-year-old girl. Private Wright was sentenced to die for his crime—but was sent to Norfolk Island instead.

With lawlessness on the increase, and robberies occurring almost every night, a convict with a life sentence, Herbert Keeling, came forward to propose that a night watch be instituted, and the governor agreed.

Twelve men were chosen to patrol the settlement, divided into four groups of three. They were on guard all night, moving from hut to hut and through the common areas, past the governor's house, the storehouses, the hospital, the cemetery, the barracks and the community garden. Herbert Keeling and his men were determined and assiduous in searching out malefactors. The judge advocate thought that the vigilante group was "of infinite utility." By late 1789 the unpaved roads of Sydney Cove, he thought, were better patrolled and safer than those of London, where the night watchmen were largely ineffectual against footpads and burglars.[6]

The Night Watch was feared and detested, especially by the soldiers, many of whom were ex-convicts, at best lax in their duties, at worst guilty of adding to the number of nightly crimes. One historian has estimated that the average battalion contained "fifty drunkards, plunderers, stragglers, and would-be deserters and criminals."[7] But Keeling and his watchmen continued to patrol through the hot weather and into early 1790, as the colony's food supplies ran low and they were faced with yet another crisis of survival.

Month by month, as Mary's pregnancy advanced, there was less and less to eat. Nine hundred hungry colonists had consumed most of the bounty brought by the *Sirius* in May. The new seeds were not yet sprouting, even at the settlement of Rose Hill—which the local tribes called Parramatta— where the soil was richer and farms had been laid out earlier in the year. Parties of marines no longer sailed to Botany Bay each week to search for a rescue ship, full of supplies, sent from England; only the most sanguine expected outside aid.[8] Weekly rations were reduced to 5 lbs. 5 oz. of flour, 3 lbs. 5 oz. of salt pork, and 3 pints of peas per person, with no exception made for pregnant women and reduced rations for the children.

Like the others, Mary foraged for wild spinach, shellfish and the herb they called sweet tea. Some wild ducks were shot, snakes and rats caught and eaten, along with the occasional lean kangaroo. But it was fish that kept the colony alive, fish that Will Bryant and others caught, and the fish in the summer of 1790 were often scarce.

The men went out every afternoon, and cast their nets into the harbor all night long. But they seldom caught more than a hundred pounds of fish—hardly enough to keep a hundred people alive, let alone nine hundred. Once in a while there would be a sudden influx of mullet or sole, bass or skate or grouper, immense schools that seemed to rush into the net and willingly entangle themselves. Then there was feasting, and a surfeit in the storehouse. But the fresh fish spoiled rapidly, and the great shoals vanished as quickly as they had appeared.

"The universal voice of all professed fishermen is," Tench wrote, "that they never fished in a country where success was so precarious and uncertain."[9]

Belts were tightened, attempts at theft from the storehouses and gardens increased, so that it took all the efforts of the Night Watch to stop them. Mary was hungry, her belly distended but her face and limbs thin under her ragged, patched clothes. She may have thought that her baby would die, she had so little to eat. She may even have wanted, or tried, to miscarry, as women commonly did by deliberate overexertion. Had she been in Cornwall she could have drunk an abortifacient, a "great dose" concocted by a woman knowledgeable in the lore of herbs. But there were no such expedients available in Sydney Cove.

The baby was alive, she could feel it kick. By January of 1790 she was seven months pregnant, ungainly and unsteady on her feet; walking was an effort and bending all but impossible. No doubt Mary tried to do her part in foraging for food, but in the hot, muggy weather she tired easily, all the more easily from being malnourished. She watched Will go out every afternoon to fish, and shared the numbing wave of disappointment that swept through the settlement when all the other fishermen returned in the morning, their nets nearly empty.

There was no longer hope for a supply ship from England, but each morning a group of seamen raised a flag on South Head, at the entrance to the harbor of Port Jackson, on the chance that a passing vessel might see their distress signal and come to their aid. And every time thunder was heard, or a musket went off, the desperate convicts shouted "A gun from a ship! A gun from a ship!" and hurried to the beach to look for a sail.[10]

On the last day of March, 1790, Mary went into labor. She was too weak to struggle for long with her pains, and the baby, when he was born, was too weak to give more than a feeble cry. She stayed awake long enough to name the tiny infant Emanuel, which in Hebrew means God with us, before falling into exhausted sleep.

Four days later Emanuel Bryant was baptized by the chaplain, the smallest and most frail of the babies in Sydney Cove, a weak little boy whose name was a prayer, an affirmation of faith in a season of famine.

XI

*T*HE LINE OF CONVICTS stretched from the door of the storehouse past the hospital and cemetery and out toward the rocky foreshore. They were waiting for their small ration of flour and salt pork, peas and butter and fish. Another reduction in the food ration had been announced, and there was anguish on every thin face.

One old man in the long line staggered as he tried to stand. "His faltering gait, and eager devouring eye, led me to watch him," Tench wrote. His face was wild and haggard, with a glassy-eyed look. It was clear to Tench that the old man was faint with hunger.

He had just received his food in his cupped hands when he fell, dropping to his knees, the precious flour and peas and fish spilling out onto the earthen floor of the storehouse. Tench ordered the old man carried to the hospital, where he died. When the surgeon opened his stomach to determine the cause of his death, it was found to be empty.[1]

The old man was only the latest in a series of starvation deaths, the numbers growing during April and May 1790. To the extreme distress caused by lack of food was added another blow. The *Sirius*, sent on another provisioning voyage in March, went aground on a reef off Norfolk Island and sank. Now no more long-range voyages for provisions were possible.

The governor, in pain from his kidney stone and gravely concerned for those under his command, had acknowledged several months earlier that "vigorous measures were become indispensable" if the colonists were to survive. But by May he had taken all the vigorous measures he could think of, and still there was far too little to eat. He had taken stock of what was left in the storehouses. With lowered rations, he calculated, and with nearly three hundred of the convicts and marines sent to Norfolk Island to find their own food, there would be enough salt meat to last until the end of June, sufficient flour to last until the middle of August, and enough rice and peas to last until the end of September. And with the numbers in Sydney Cove dwindling by the day from starvation, the meager rations might last even longer.

These were grim calculations indeed. Famine "was approaching with gigantic strides," Tench wrote, "and gloom and dejection overspread every countenance. Men abandoned themselves to the most desponding reflections, and adopted the most extravagant conjectures."[2] Words failed Tench as he tried to convey the general depression. "The misery and horror of such a situation cannot be imparted, even by those who have suffered under it."

What the colonists could not know was that a naval storeship, the *Guardian*, had been on its way to them when it struck an iceberg off the Cape of Good Hope and sank.[3] They had not been abandoned after all, but fate and the peril of the seas had deprived them of the supplies they badly needed.

In desperation Governor Phillip decided to send the *Supply* to the Dutch colony of Batavia (modern Indonesia) for emergency supplies of food. The monsoon season had begun, the *Supply* would likely have rough sailing. On the day she left, April 17, 1790, the colonists watched her departure anxiously, waving and calling out weak cries of Godspeed. The *Supply* carried the hope of Port Jackson with her; no one could say how many of those who gathered in dismal groups on the beach to watch her go would still be alive on her return—*if* she returned.

In the meantime, all energies had to be applied to the single overarching task of gathering food. A hunting party was sent out, made up of the most capable marksmen, to shoot kangaroos. All the able-bodied men went fishing every night, even the surgeons and the chaplain, and every boat, "public and private," Tench wrote, was commandeered to join the modest fishing fleet.

Because of their extra exertions, the hunters and fishermen were given a small additional portion of flour and salt pork—but this meant that there was even less food for the rest of the convicts and marines, and especially for the women and children.

The salt pork, which by April 1790 was nearly four years old, was only marginally fit to eat. It was so old and dry that, when boiled, it shrivelled to half its size. Toasted on a fork, it yielded a few drops of fat, which were caught on a slice of bread or in a saucer of rice and eaten greedily. Compared to fresh fish, the pork gave little nourishment.[4] Yet the fish remained elusive. Some days the nets were full, but most days the catch was thin, with a daily average of only sixty fish altogether.[5] And only three small kangaroos were shot. Were it not for the remains of the flour brought from Cape Town on the *Sirius* a year earlier, far more of the convicts would have died that fall.

Half-starved though she herself was, Mary suckled her tiny son, and wrapped him as warmly as she could in patchwork blankets made of odd scraps of cloth pieced together. He did not thrive, but he did not die either, as so many of the colony's babies and young children did, and by the end of May he was two months old. Charlotte, now two and a half, was lethargic from constant hunger and growing thinner, living as she now did on the common children's ration of a pound of salt pork every week plus a bit of flour and rice.

Each day there was less to eat, less to hope for, more hunger and cold and more suffering.

With each bleak new dawn the fishermen came back from their long nights of labor, tired from having hauled in their near-empty nets. During the morning news of more deaths passed through the camp—deaths of friends, of friends' children, of pitiable acquaintances. During the day there were funerals, and burials—the shovelling of earth in the cemetery seemed to go on constantly. There were also punishments. The Night Watch caught a convict stealing potatoes from the chaplain's garden. He was given three hundred lashes, then sentenced to be deprived of his flour ration for six months. (The governor soon relented, however, knowing that without his flour ration the man would die; the ration was restored.)[6] After the sparse portions of fish were distributed, the settlers ate their minuscule daily meal of pork, fish, rice (each grain of rice, Tench thought, "a moving body"), boiled flour with scurvy grass and fern roots. Then they lay down hungry, shivering in the cold, the children crying, the convicts swearing, quarrels and hostilities erupting on all sides from sheer frustration and deprivation.

Late into the night, the talk in the huts, in the barracks, in the governor's brick house and in Sodom was of food, and the shortage of food, and the dismal prospects for rescue. Everyone knew that it was too late in the sailing season for a ship from England to arrive in Port Jackson. The winds were wrong, the seas far too treacherous. The *Supply* might or might not return from Batavia. If it did, the return could be months away.

In the Bryants' hut the talk was of food, and food shortages, and of the contrary winds and the bleak sailing season. But there was also talk of a plan that was taking shape, a bold plan, one that would require great daring and entail great risk.

There was talk of escape.

Mary and Will and three friends met frequently to discuss how it might be possible to get away from Port Jackson and take their freedom. One of the three was James Martin, the black-haired Irishman who had been convicted at Exeter Assizes along with Mary, had been on the prison hulk *Dunkirk* with her, and had made the journey to New Holland with Mary and Will aboard the *Charlotte*. Martin was in his late twenties, a little above average height and of an enterprising nature. Like Will, he was literate, and in 1790 he was some four years into his seven-year sentence. James Martin had shared the Bryants' hardships for a long time; now he meant to share their attempt at freedom.[7]

The second of the trio of friends, James Cox or "Banbury Jack," was serving out a sentence of transportation for life for stealing some thread lace—almost certainly one of many crimes he had committed. Cox may have been a leading planner of the escape; he had daring and courage, as future events were to show. Of his age and appearance nothing is known, but his dashing nickname suggests a strong persona, with a certain mystique. Banbury Jack was a man to be reckoned with—and a strong partner in the Bryants' plans.[8]

The third of the trio of friends, Samuel Bird of Croydon, is the most shadowy. He had been convicted, with his brother John, in July of 1785, of breaking into a warehouse and stealing a thousand pounds of saltpeter—a component of gunpowder, and a valuable commodity. (The Birds' thousand pounds of saltpeter were worth thirty pounds, a very large sum in the 1780s.) Both brothers were sentenced to seven years' transportation, and both came to Port Jackson on the First Fleet. Beyond that, little is known of Sam Bird— and nothing of his brother. Had John Bird perished in the famine? Or was he ill, or disinclined to discuss escape? Perhaps he had had a falling out with Sam, or with Will Bryant. Or perhaps John Bird had escape plans of his own. In any case, only Sam pledged himself to join the venture that was taking shape.

Mary, Will, James, Sam and Banbury Jack: they would get away, as best they could, as soon as they could, before they starved.

Shouting and the sound of running feet along the main street of Sydney Cove brought everyone out into the cold evening of June 3, 1790. In the sunset light the lookout flag had been glimpsed. A ship had been sighted.

It had been raining all day, a driving, tempestuous rain, and the colonists who ran down to the beach, hugging one another wetly and kissing their children and crying for joy, were soon soaked to the skin, their bare feet caked with mud.

"The flag's up! The flag's up!" they cried out again and again.

Captain Tench—he had been promoted to captain—snatched up his spyglass and immediately ran to the nearest hill, another officer following him. From the top the two men could clearly see, through the squally clouds, a large ship flying English colors, making her way through the harbor entrance.

"We could not speak," Tench wrote. "We wrung each other by the hand, with eyes and hearts overflowing."[9] They had all been wrong in thinking no ship would arrive so late in the sailing season. For here was this vessel—as she came closer, they made out the word "London" on her stern—that had come halfway around the world in spite of storms and contrary winds, icebergs and mountainous seas. Providence had not abandoned them. They had been spared.

The governor got into his cutter and had himself rowed out toward the harbor entrance to meet the incoming ship, a few fishing boats following in the cutter's wake. Tench had taken his place in the cutter, eager to be among the first to welcome the vessel. The closer they came to the large ship, the more worried they got; the ship appeared at first to be in danger ("we were in agony," Tench recalled), but then seemed to be holding her own against a strong southerly wind that made it difficult for her to progress up the harbor.

The oarsmen in the cutter pulled with all their strength, disregarding the rain, which continued to shower down, causing the men to have to bail.

"Pull away, my lads! She is from Old England!"

"A few strokes more, and we shall be aboard!"

"Hurrah for a belly-full, and news from our friends!"

They read her name: *Lady Juliana.* A transport. She would be one of several ships, there had to be more coming. Surely an entire flotilla was on its way into Port Jackson, of which this vessel was only the first.

Crew and passengers were shouting and waving, the men in the cutter answering in kind. Governor Phillip, realizing the enormity of what he was seeing, and the challenges to come, with so many people arriving for whom no accommodation had been prepared, got out of the cutter and into one of the attendant fishing boats, and had himself rowed back to Sydney Cove at once. Tench and the others, however, approached the ship and went aboard.

The first thing they saw was an immense crowd of women, ragged-looking and in chains, many with an unhealthy pallor, staring down at them from the deck. They were a tough-looking group—in fact they had given the marines and crew aboard the *Lady Juliana* a very hard time during the voyage, as the memoirs of their steward, John Nicol, were to attest. Jubilant, cocky, defiant, the women stood on deck, arms akimbo, some with pipes in their mouths, sizing up the marines from Sydney Cove as they pulled closer and came aboard.

Amid the excitement there came a clamor of questions from Tench and the others. How long had the *Lady Juliana* been at sea? Did she carry any letters for the settlement at Port Jackson? What was the news from England? How many more ships were coming? What news of La Pérouse and his ships, which had left Botany Bay two years earlier? Had La Pérouse carried two escapees from Port Jackson on board?

"We continued to ask a thousand questions on a breath," wrote Tench, while letters were torn open eagerly and their contents devoured.

No, the marines were told by the *Lady Juliana*'s captain, Captain Aitken, La Pérouse had not been heard from.[10] There were four ships in the *Lady Juliana*'s fleet, with over a thousand convicts plus crew and marines.

The *Lady Juliana*, the crew told Tench and the others, had been at sea in all a year minus one day. They had called in at Tenerife and St. Jago and Rio and Cape Town, and had made their run from Cape Town in seventy-five days. They had nearly come to grief when one of the ship's carpenters overturned a pot of boiling pitch on deck, starting a fire. But the steward had thrown a blanket over the fire and it hadn't spread.

As far as events in the larger world, there had been a revolution in France, and the king had been put in his place. And the English King George, God bless him, had been very ill but was now well again, according to the latest news to reach Cape Town. The *Guardian* had sunk on its way to Port Jackson, loaded with supplies.

And there was another remarkable piece of news. Captain William Bligh, late of HMS *Bounty*, had been relieved of command during a mutiny in April of the previous year, 1789, in the Friendly Isles and had managed to sail all the way to Batavia in a twenty-three-foot launch with eighteen of his crew. Who had ever heard of such a thing![11] A journey of upwards of four thousand miles across open ocean in such a small vessel.

Tench and his companions listened with the greatest interest, astounded by all the news from the distant outside world, as the *Lady Juliana* tried in vain to sail up the harbor to Sydney Cove amid the hard southerly wind and pelting rain.

XII

ONCE AGAIN THERE WAS FOOD, abundant food, flour and beef, salt pork and rice, salt and tea and sugar— along with tobacco and spirits. Not only did the *Lady Juliana* bring food, but a storeship, the *Justinian*, soon arrived on June 20, 1790, with hundreds of tons of provisions. And there was cloth, and needles and thread, which the convicts had not had for three years. During their voyage the women aboard the *Lady Juliana* had been given the task of sewing shirts for the male convicts. Once the ship was unloaded, the shirts were distributed or sold, and Mary and the other convict women were allowed enough rough cloth to make themselves new dresses and aprons, and to clothe their children. Charlotte and Emanuel had new smocks, Will a new shirt. The tattered old clothes were torn into strips to make blankets.

Food and clothing, new companions—and hope. For a few brief weeks in the antipodean winter of 1790, the convicts' dissatisfactions were tempered by satiety and a measure of comfort.

Then on June 26 the *Surprize*, a small transport, sailed into Port Jackson and began to offload her wretched human cargo.

There were some two hundred convicts, many of them skeletal wretches too weak to move, their starved bodies encrusted with feces and vomit, suffering from scurvy and boils and swarming with lice.

The colony's chaplain, Richard Johnson, went among them, his face white with shock at the sight of their appalling condition. He was accustomed to the look of starving men, as everyone in Port Jackson was. He had prayed at the bedsides of many dying men and women during his years of service aboard the First Fleet and in Port Jackson, and had presided at untold numbers of funerals.

But the death-in-life of the denizens of the *Surprize* stunned him. He was horror-stricken, carried past shock, all but speechless. He had not known such a level of human misery existed.

"I beheld a sight truly shocking to the feelings of humanity," he wrote after going aboard the *Surprize*. "A great number of them [the convicts] laying, some half and others nearly quite naked, without either bed or bedding, unable to turn or help themselves. Spoke to them as I passed along, but the smell was so offensive that I could scarcely bear it."

When two larger transport ships arrived two days later, the immense *Neptune*, a vessel of eight hundred tons, and the four-hundred-ton *Scarborough* (a veteran of the First Fleet, making her second voyage to Port Jackson), Chaplain Johnson's shock deepened. The nearly four hundred convicts on these ships were "still more wretched and intolerable." When they landed, "great numbers were not able to walk, nor to move hand or foot; such were slung over the ship's side in the same manner as they would sling a cask, a box or anything of that nature."

When brought up onto the deck from the wet, dark prison of the hold, "some fainted, some died upon the deck, and others [died] in the boat before they reached the shore."

There seemed no end to the ghastly spectacle. Convicts, seamen and marines crowded around to help the starveling men (nearly all were men, the convict women having come on the *Lady Juliana*), the surgeons assisting as many as they could, but overwhelmed by the sheer numbers of the sufferers.

"When come on shore," Johnson wrote, "many were not able to walk, to stand, or to stir themselves in the least, hence some were led by others. Some creeped upon their hands and knees, and some were carried upon the backs of others."[1]

All the women in the colony, Mary among them, were immediately ordered to nurse the ill and dying. It was a futile and depressing task, made more depressing and more stressful by the vast numbers of the suffering. There were far too many sick and dying men for the already overcrowded hospital to accommodate. Thirty tents were put up as a crude hospital annex, the men laid on blankets on the cold ground or over mounds of dried leaves. While the wind tore at the fragile tents and rain came down through the roof, Mary and the other women did what they could to clean and comfort and soothe their patients, offering food and water, wiping away the fetid matter, keeping vigil over the dying, helpless to save them. For in most cases it was too late, they were too far gone to respond. Some of the starving gorged until their stomachs burst, killing them. Others could not retain the food and water they were given, their shrunken stomachs vomited it up. Those with grave cases of scurvy could drink, but did not thrive, and died of infection. Glassy-eyed, shivering, moaning in anguish, the convicts died in their hundreds, and were buried hastily, in rain-sodden pits, with the ashen-faced Reverend Johnson repeating Bible verses of hope and reciting the traditional Anglican prayers.

"In the midst of life we are in death," he intoned at the daily funerals, and for everyone in Sydney Cove, the chilling observation must have taken on new meaning. For they were indeed in death, and in peril of death, that winter. Stricken by what they witnessed daily, alternately numbed, shocked and sickened and filled with an affecting sorrow, the surviving convicts thought about their own bleak future, and tried not to give in to despair.

In the Bryants' hut, the catastrophe of the Second Fleet was a spur to the burgeoning escape plan. Mary and Will, James Martin, Sam Bird and Banbury Jack Cox were more convinced than ever that their only hope of surviving was to try to get away—far away, so far that they would be beyond the reach of Governor Phillip or of English justice.

And they would have to go soon, before the food supply dwindled to near-nothing once again. Before the arrival of the next fleet of convict ships, which they were told was already on its way. Before the land, which by July and August had begun to dry out, could be utterly denuded of vegetation by drought. And before the next storm season set in, in the southern fall, at the end of March.

They had seven months or so—if the food held out. By then they would need to go.

The story of Captain Bligh and his remarkable thirty-five-hundred-mile voyage across the Pacific to Timor, the easternmost settlement of the Dutch East Indies, must have encouraged the Bryants and their colleagues greatly. Bligh had a small open boat, a launch. He had a compass and a quadrant—and his memory of the Pacific waters, for he had sailed them with Captain Cook. And he was, by all accounts, a brilliant navigator. Above all, Bligh and his eighteen companions had the predictable, reliable southeast monsoon, to push them steadily westward.

If Bligh and his men could accomplish their journey, why could not the Bryants accomplish a similar journey, making their way northward along the eastern coast of New Holland until they too reached the tropical northern waters—waters that, as yet, had no name—that led to Batavia? Even now, in the winter of 1790, the *Supply* had taken this route—as Captain Cook had taken it years earlier. When the *Supply* returned, her captain and crew would have much to tell about the coastline and its features—and its hazards.

All they needed was a boat, and some provisions, good sailing weather and the courage to seize their opportunity.

And, of course, a navigator. Will was an experienced seaman, but he had never navigated a long voyage. A navigator was essential; one would have to be found, and persuaded to join in the escape venture.

The arrival of the Second Fleet wrought a sea change in Port Jackson; with their coming a new air of desperation and resolution swept through the settlement as it coped with the catastrophe of mass death. Survivors of the Second Fleet were exceptionally hardened, having been winnowed out; they alone were tough enough to have withstood the punishing rigors of the voyage and its deadly aftermath. They had been starved, beaten and abused by exploitative ship's masters and guards. They had made the voyage, many of them, in irons, with water up to their waists a good deal of the time.[2] They had been chained to dead men, and had been glad to eat the rations apportioned to those who had died. And they had managed, at the last, to cheat death after coming ashore, even as so many of their companions succumbed.

Physically vigorous, psychologically hardy, the Second Fleeters were exceptionally strong and robust—and more than ready to hazard their further survival on bold ventures.

They had been trying to escape, in small groups of three or four, from the outset of their voyage. On the night before the *Lady Juliana* left Portsmouth, four of the women convicts aboard had escaped with the aid of friends ashore. They created a diversion, pretending to be drunk, singing and laughing. They drew the watchman on the quarterdeck into the carousal, giving him so much gin that he eventually passed out. Then the four women quietly went over the side and dropped down a makeshift ladder to a waiting boat that took them ashore. The escapees were not missed; the *Lady Juliana* sailed without them, and only when she was well on her way to Tenerife did the guards discover that there were four fewer convicts aboard.[3]

Only four months before the *Scarborough* landed in Port Jackson, a number of the convicts had plotted a mutiny.[4] They knew that the crew of the *Bounty* had succeeded in taking over their ship and expelling the captain; they may have had dreams of seizing the *Scarborough* and sailing her to the Friendly Isles, where they could live out their lives in the warm tropics amid the comforts of fragrant breezes and hospitable islanders. The *Scarborough* mutineers plotted to murder their officers rather than set them adrift, as those in the *Bounty* had done. Beyond the gaining of their freedom, revenge was no doubt their primary motive, revenge for all they had suffered.

But an eavesdropper, or one of the plotters themselves,

disclosed the conspiracy to the guards, and all the conspirators were seized and punished. The ringleaders were flogged, the most dangerous of them "stapled to the deck"—an excruciating torture—and there was no more overt rebellion on the ship for the remainder of the voyage.

Soon after the Second Fleet landed, the pace of escape attempts quickened. One convict "perished in the woods," probably attempting to get away by going overland. Seven others drowned, possibly through misadventure, but equally possibly while trying to row down the harbor to the sea—or swim to safety. When the *Neptune* sailed for Canton at the end of August, it was discovered that two men and a woman had stowed away among the firewood; they were taken ashore and punished.[5] And two convicts simply disappeared; probably they stowed away successfully on one of the transports.

In September of 1790 a convict named John Tarwood from the Second Fleet, "a daring, desperate character," according to Judge Advocate Collins, led four others in a bold dash for the sea and freedom.[6] Starting from the small settlement at Rose Hill (Parramatta), the men rowed a punt downriver at night, past Sydney Cove, continued on to South Head where they stole a small oared boat with a sail used by the lookout. They managed to avoid the hazards of the heads and sailed out into the open ocean. They did not return.

In the Bryants' hut, the escape of John Tarwood and his colleagues, among them one Joseph Sutton, who had tried in vain to stow away on the *Neptune* when she left Port Jackson a month earlier, must have been the subject of endless conversations. How had they done it? How had they managed to steal the punt, to elude the guards at Rose Hill and slip past the Night Watch at Sydney Cove? To seize the lookout boat and get away without being shot at and apprehended? Tarwood had been overheard to say that he meant to sail to Tahiti, four thousand miles away. Was this possible? Were the winds right in September for sailing eastward?

It was said Tarwood and the others had planned their escape for months, hoarding food, gathering fishing tackle. They had tried to get muskets and pistols but without success. How much food and water would they have needed to get to Tahiti?

Beyond the questions and the constant analysis, Mary and Will and their friends must have imagined John Tarwood and the others out at sea, on their way across the vast Pacific, riding out storms, facing the hardships of exposure and food shortages, making their way mile by mile into the unknown.

It was possible, they had to believe it: a handful of people in a small boat could travel thousands of miles. With a sound boat and adequate provisions, luck and fortitude—and a skilled navigator.

When four more would-be escapees, all from the Second Fleet, joined the Bryants and their friends in the winter of 1790, one of them, William Morton, was just the man they had been looking for.

Nothing is known of Morton but this: that he was able, given a compass and quadrant, charts and reasonably good visibility, to steer a boat toward a predetermined destination. And that he was bold enough, and desperate enough, to want to join in the escape plan.

Of the second member of the new quartet of escapees, Nathaniel Lilley, much more is known. He was an Irishman, thirty-seven years old, at five feet eight inches nearly as tall as James Martin, with black hair and grey eyes. He had been convicted of theft; he broke into the house of one Benjamin Summersett and stole a fishnet, a watch and two spoons.

He could have been hanged. However, "there being favorable circumstances in his case," the judge reprieved him on condition that he serve a term of seven years transportation to New Holland.[7] What the "favorable circumstances" were is unknown. In 1790 Lilley was in the third year of his seven-year term.

Tall, strong John Butcher, a farm laborer from Worcestershire, was the third of the new recruits to join the Bryants. He was forty-eight years old, with sandy hair that had not yet turned grey and a ruddy complexion. Sentenced to seven years' transportation for stealing three small pigs, Butcher prided himself on his agricultural expertise. Having been, in his own words, brought up "in the thorough knowledge of all kinds of land and capable of bringing indifferent lands to perfection," Butcher was not at all knowledgeable about the ocean, but could learn. Meanwhile his strength and stamina—and his self-confidence—could be useful on a long voyage.[8]

At fifty-three the senior member of the group, William Allen, was a Yorkshireman from Hull, and a seaman. Tall and dark, his skin creased and brown from years in the sun, Allen was a violent criminal, convicted of theft; he had robbed a shop, apparently using force and possibly armed with a knife or pistol. He was in the fourth year of his seven-year sentence.

They met, the nine of them, in the Bryants' hut in the evening, and they made their plans and preparations. Whether their discussions were long and full of argument or brief and efficient is not known. However, they did not manage to keep their planning a secret. They were spied on, and reported—perhaps by the Night Watch, perhaps by the disloyal Joseph Paget—to the marine guards, who informed the governor and his staff.

The nine were watched, but not apprehended or formally charged. Most likely there were many such clusters of convicts, meeting when and where they could, plotting escape. Not all could be pursued or brought before the judge advocate. Besides, the colony's authorities were preoccupied with more pressing concerns in the second half of 1790. There were so many more convicts to provide for, and hundreds more would soon be arriving. That meant more shelter, more storehouses, more bricks to be made—the convicts working at the brick kilns were turning out tens of thousands of bricks a month—more of everything. Of those convicts who had survived the terrible mortality of the winter months, many were too weak to work, and had to be nursed and fed. Even with the portable hospital brought by the *Justinian* finally in place, there were not enough beds, and more shelter for the sick and weak was a high priority. Among the ill was Governor Phillip, whose kidney stones caused him severe pain.

With the governor ill, many of the officials disheartened and the prospect of even more strain, overwork and anxieties to come, the governing of Sydney Cove may have been lax toward the end of 1790. The plotting of would-be escapees, as long as it was only plotting, could be tolerated.

For Mary, continuing to nurse the sick, relieved that her daughter and baby son were thriving, the escape plan offered hope. She may have been its instigator; almost certainly she was a major force in bringing it about. From all that is known about Mary—former highwaywoman, hardy survivor of hazards at sea, wife and mother, her husband's partner in dishonest distribution of the fish he caught—she was a woman who seized her opportunities and held on tenaciously. She had drive, and strength of purpose.

And now her hope was expanding.

On October 18, 1790, the *Supply* returned safely from Batavia, and the mariners aboard had a remarkable tale to tell. On their way to and from Batavia, they had sailed all the way around New Holland—something no European but Captain Cook had ever done before them—and they had experienced for themselves the winds, currents and waters surrounding the vast continent. They had seen the remarkable green color of the Indian Ocean—so unlike the deep sapphire blue of the Pacific—and had felt the hot winds off the Nullarbor Plain (as it would later be known) in the Great Australian Bight. They had sweated in the humid, tropical north and admired the lush, broad-leaved plants, aquamarine beaches and fish-filled shallows of the Great Barrier Reef.

It had not been an easy journey. While at Batavia, many of the ship's company had been taken ill with malaria. Some had died, others had been left in the dirty, overcrowded hospital, in expectation of death. A few in the crew who had caught the fever and survived, skeletal and jaundiced, to describe their ordeal made it back to Sydney Cove; their ravaged faces and weakened bodies showed how devastating the fever could be, and how long it took for even the luckiest of its victims to be restored to normal life and health.[9]

Still, with the successful return of the *Supply*, more was known about the coast of New Holland—the entire coast—and no doubt the nine would-be escapees picked up what information they could from the ship's crew. They were confident, they had a growing expectation of success. "After the escape of Captain Bligh," Tench wrote, "which was well known to us, no length of passage, or hazard of navigation, seemed above human accomplishment."[10]

Amid these sanguine hopes, in the last days of 1790, at the start of summer, the Dutch ship *Waaksamheyd*, a small, broad-bottomed square-rigged ship filled with beef and salt pork, flour and sugar and rice, sailed into Port Jackson after a journey of three months and anchored in the roads off Sydney Cove.

XIII

*T*HE NAME *Waaksamheyd*, in Dutch, means "Watch-
fulness," and the captain of the newest ship to enter
Sydney Harbor, Detmer Smith, was certainly watchful of his financial interests.

The English judged Captain Smith to be greedy and mercenary. When during his stay in Batavia Captain Ball of the
Supply had negotiated with Smith for the hire of the
Waaksamheyd, the Dutchman drove a very hard bargain.
And when Governor Phillip tried to hire the *Waaksamheyd*
to take himself and a number of seamen and marines back to
England, Captain Smith at first quoted a price of three hundred and thirty pounds—an outrageously high sum—before
lowering his fee to a more realistic level.

Smith was not only mercenary, he was dishonest. The
provisions he brought into Sydney Cove were found to be

old and spoiled, the rice full of weevils, the pork "ill-flavored, rusty and smoked." All the provisions were weighed on landing (much to the disgust of the ship's master, a crusty and ill-mannered character whom the English found to be "very disagreeable" and "impertinent"), and it was discovered that the weevil-ridden rice was some forty-three thousand pounds less than had been paid for. An extra ton of butter was demanded as compensation.

The Dutch were tired and out of sorts; they had had a long and dangerous voyage, battling contrary winds and losing sixteen of the Malay crewmen to accidents and disease. It was no wonder the ship's master was snappish and irritable, and Captain Smith fuming and stubborn in his negotiations with Governor Phillip.

For if the English thought the Dutch were churlish and deceitful, the Dutch considered the English officers to be arrogant and self-righteous, full of themselves and afflicted with hauteur.

That the two groups were at odds was to the advantage of the Bryants. When Will approached Captain Smith, offering to buy from him the supplies and equipment he and his friends needed in order to make an escape attempt, the Dutchman agreed. Smith was hostile to the English authorities; why shouldn't he sell a compass and quadrant to Will and Mary and their confederates, along with a little flour and rice and pork? Why shouldn't he give them a chart of the coast, and sit down with Will and his friend Will Morton and tell them what he knew of the coastal waters?

Captain Smith even sold the escapees several muskets and a supply of powder—a very risky decision indeed, given who the purchasers were and the captain's own relative vulnerability.

With Smith's information about winds and tides, and

with a chart—however sketchy and inaccurate—along with a hundred pounds of flour and the same of rice, fourteen pounds of "rusty" pork and a quantity of sweet tea leaves, plus a supply of nails, rope, a grapnel for use as an anchor, some carpenter's tools, a fishing net and line and some resin and beeswax for caulking the seams of the boat and the all-important weapons, the Bryants were on their way to being equipped for their journey.

They would go in the governor's cutter, a small open boat some twenty-three feet long and about seven feet wide with a mast and lugsail.[1] During January and February of 1791 Will and the others made repairs and alterations to the cutter, ostensibly to improve her for fishing but actually making her ready for a long voyage. They fitted her with new masts and oars and made new flax sails for her. Will altered her, adding beds, probably aft, and strengthening her planking. The cutter had been in near-constant use for the past four years, a re-fitting was long overdue.

The challenge of the undertaking was extreme, and none in the escape party doubted it. Not only would they be setting off for the unknown, encountering unforeseen hazards and unexpected dangers, but they would be leaving at or close to the onset of the season when the southeast monsoon brought storms and heavy seas. They might founder and drown, or be eaten by sharks or stung by poisonous goblin fish of the kind that infested the harbor of Port Jackson. They might run aground on a reef, or be driven onshore by winds and currents and dashed against sharp rocks. They might be caught in a whirlpool, or carried upwards by cyclonic winds, or sunk by a breaching whale.

They would not be able to carry much water, and would have to go ashore frequently to replenish their supply. As for food, they hoped there would be plenty of fish when the supplies of flour and rice and pork ran out. They all knew the risks of disease, and of exposure to severe weather; they had all experienced these, and lived through them.

They knew the risks. With what varying degrees of fortitude or trepidation they faced them, their great and overwhelming desire was to get away, and this desire took precedence over all else.

The summer of 1791 was the most extreme the colonists had yet experienced. A scalding wind from the northwest made the air so hot and dry that grass burst into flame. Brush fires threatened Sydney Cove and Rose Hill, and with the water in the streams very low, it was difficult to put the fires out once they started. Convicts were put to work deepening the streambeds, but by midmorning of each working day they were wilting and fainting in the heat; by midafternoon the temperature was at 105 or 106 degrees near the harbor, and even hotter inland. As happened every summer, birds fell to the parched ground in midflight and lay where they fell, gasping for water. Plants in all the gardens shrivelled and died, and in the woods, fires flared, spread, and eventually burned themselves out.

It was a season for lethargy, but in the Bryants' hut, secret activity continued. Supplies for the coming journey were hidden in a cache under the floor. Meetings were held, decisions made about when to leave and how to manage the loading and launching of the boat without detection. The unmarried convicts said their private good-byes to sweethearts and lovers, and to their closest friends.

When and to whom Mary said her good-byes is nowhere recorded. She must have made friends among the women convicts—and perhaps enemies and rivals. Possibly Catherine Fryer and Mary Haydon, her two confederates from Exeter, were still alive and living in Sydney Cove. There must have been many in the cemetery, men and women alike, whom she had known, nursed and mourned. But those closest to her, Will and her children, would be with her wherever she went; there was no need to say good-bye to them. Or to the seven men who had become her comrades and fellow conspirators in recent months.

On the strength and skill of these seven men, plus her husband, and on her own fortitude, Mary was about to risk her future safety and that of her children. A sobering thought indeed—if she took the time to reflect on it. But Mary's time was taken up by activity, not reflection, as Sydney Cove baked in the terrible searing heat of high summer, and the time for departure came closer with each passing day.

By the end of February, 1791, the group was almost ready to go. The secret cache was nearly full of food and equipment, work on the boat was done. Will took the cutter out into the harbor fishing, with a crew of convicts and others aboard. He caught what fish he could, then hoisted the sail and began to tack up the harbor, the boat heavily laden with fish and with her human cargo and lying low in the water.

Then something unexpected happened. A strong gust of wind filled the sail and, before Will could go about, the sail was torn away from the mast and the boat filled with water and keeled over. The crew and few passengers swam to safety, but Will, wanting above all to save the cutter on which all the escape plans depended, stayed with the capsized boat, trying to right her, even as the current carried her toward the rocks.

Several of the Ioras, witnessing the accident from on shore, came to Will's rescue and saved both Will and his vessel, gathering up the oars and other pieces of flotsam from the near-wreck and towing the damaged cutter up to the cove.[2]

Will was not injured, but the boat was badly damaged—so badly that all plans for escape had to be abandoned for the time being.

Over the next month the needed repairs were made, new planking put in place and a new mast made and sails sewn. Outwardly, the cutter was once again sound—as sound as she had been before the accident. But the damage to Will's self-confidence, and to the hopes of Mary and the others, must have been equally hard to repair. For the accident had been a reminder of just how precarious the long sea journey would be, how vulnerable the vessel, how helpless the passengers when confronted by sudden gusts and rogue waves. All must have wondered how seaworthy the repaired cutter truly was, how difficult she would be to maneuver in rough waters.

Still, peril or no peril, they were committed to the venture. Soon the weather would change, they had to go quickly, and on a night of no moon and a calm sea.

All the transports had left the harbor, the *Supply* had been sent to Norfolk Island and there was only the *Waaksamheyd* lying at anchor off Sydney Cove. On March 27, 1791, the Dutch ship sailed for England. Now the authorities lacked the means to give chase to any escaping vessel, even if the escape should be discovered; once the cutter was far down the harbor, none of the smaller fishing craft had the speed to catch her.

On the moonless night of March 28, sometime between nine and midnight, Mary and Will, James Martin and Sam Bird and Banbury Jack, Will Morton, Nate Lilley, John Butcher and Will Allen quietly left the Bryants' hut, hauling their sacks of flour and rice, flagons of water, muskets and powder and bags of tools. They must have made several trips out to the beach where the cutter was tethered, carrying no light, groping their way along the familiar path, swearing under their breaths when they stumbled. In their haste they dropped a scale and a handsaw, and spilled several pounds of rice. But no one noticed or reported them.

With every quiet step they must have been listening for the Night Watch, and for the bells that struck the hour, and for the reassuring voices of the sentinels at their posts calling out "All's well." The encampment was asleep by the time the two children, Charlotte and Emanuel, were brought from the hut and put into the boat, and the six strongest men began to pull at the oars.

The tide was with them as they rowed down the harbor toward South Head, where the sentries were, and the wind favorable. The only sounds, in the stillness of the night, were the regular slap of the oars in the water and the gurgle of small waves passing under the cutter's bow. They rowed for hours, taking turns at the oars, until to their great relief they passed safely out through the harbor mouth, pursued by no hue and cry from the sentries. By dawn they were nearly out of sight of land, scudding along under dark rain clouds, riding the swells of the open ocean.

XIV

*T*HE RAIN CAME DOWN in hard drops, then in sheets, soaking everyone and everything. They huddled together on the thwarts, trying in vain to stay dry and keep the provisions dry, Mary doing her best to shield the children from the rain and the spray that came up over the bow.

The cutter rode low in the water, and being heavy, was hard to steer. Will, at the tiller, did his best to keep her headed into the oncoming swells, but with each wave the cutter swerved and had to be righted, her movement sluggish. Navigator Will Morton read the damp chart and watched the coast, looking for each headland and hill and attempting to match what he glimpsed with what was marked in ink. But the coast was hard to see; not only did the constant rise and fall of the boat make it appear to bounce and tilt, but the rain obscured it and made it seem farther away and of indeterminate shape.

The winds blew steadily from the northeast, bringing the rain and making it hard to go ashore. But by the third day the travellers had no choice but to land; the boat was leaking and they needed to repair it and to refill their water flagons.

"After two days' sail [we] reached a little creek about two degrees to the northward of Port Jackson [and] there found a quantity of fine burning coal," James Martin wrote in the brief account he later wrote of the voyage.[1] The wind had changed, now it was against them, blowing down the coast from the north. The monsoon had set in. They had waited too long to leave Sydney Cove.

Still, when they entered the mouth of the small creek and dragged the boat up the bank, they found the area to be more fertile and hospitable than Port Jackson. "The appearance of the land appears more better here than at Sydney Cove," Martin recalled. Will threw out the seine net and hauled in a large quantity of grey mullet and other fish, which they cooked over a fire made of coals they found on the beach. With the mullet they ate the leaves of "cabbage trees" they felled—the first greens they had eaten since leaving Sydney Cove.

"The natives came down," Martin wrote, "to which we gave some clothes and other articles and they went away much satisfied." When the leaking seams of the cutter had been caulked with rosin and beeswax, and the flagons were filled with fresh water, the group left the place they called "Fortunate Cove" on March 31—baby Emanuel's first birthday—and sailed northward.

They were well on their way; no one from Port Jackson appeared to be following them. On they went up the deeply serrated coast, past coves and inlets and beaches lashed by fierce high surf. By April 1 they were, by Will's reckoning, at latitude 33 degrees—about halfway between Sydney Cove and modern Brisbane—and were looking for a safe harbor once again, for the cutter was again leaking badly. On April 2, in the afternoon, they sighted an exceptionally large harbor and took refuge there. Once again they dragged the boat up on shore and applied fresh coats of rosin and beeswax to her seams, and filled their flagons with fresh water.

But they had no sooner finished these tasks when they were "driven off by the natives," as Martin wrote, "who meant to destroy us." These were naked, copper-colored men with spears and bark canoes, aggressive and hostile. The convicts launched the cutter and made for the inner harbor, and the next day made another attempt to land farther up the coast. But they had hardly unloaded the boat when once more a party of aboriginals appeared "in vast numbers with spears and shields" and they were forced to defend themselves.

"One party of us made towards them the better by signs to pacify them," Martin recalled later. "But they were not taking the least notice. Accordingly we fired a musket thinking to affright them. But they took not the least notice thereof."[2]

The convicts took to their heels, rushed to their boat and got in. After conferring hastily together—for the group had no leader, and made decisions by consensus—they rowed up the harbor some ten miles until they reached a small sandy island. The hostile aboriginals not having followed, the escapees caulked the cutter yet again and did their best to repair her bottom, using what limited materials they had, and rested for two days.

It was still raining; there had been no letup since they left

Sydney Cove. Autumn had set in, the wind had become fickle, shifting unpredictably. When next they took to sea there was a sudden change in the weather, a strong offshore breeze driving them so far out to sea that they lost sight of land completely. They managed, with some difficulty, to tack back closer to shore, but a high surf made inshore sailing dangerous, and for the next several weeks they were unable to land anywhere.

"For near three weeks we were much distressed for water and wood," Martin wrote. They gathered up all the rainfall they could, and wrung the water out of their clothes and drank it and lapped the drops of rain that fell on their salt-encrusted limbs. But there was barely enough to wet their parched tongues. They knew better than to try to drink sea-water; it only worsened thirst. They looked with longing at the clouds that hung low over the hills along the coast, fat grey rainclouds that piled up each afternoon and watered the land. They imagined cool streams, waterfalls, deep clear pools overhung by moss-covered trees. But the twenty-foot waves that rolled in to crash on the beaches and against the rocks made landing impossible—and besides, they feared another attack by a local tribe.

Eventually two of the strongest swimmers among the men, watching for a brief cessation in the high surf, swam ashore with the water casks—only to be frightened back into the surf again by great numbers of tribesmen. They returned to the cutter with no water and only a little wood.

By now Mary and Will and their companions had been at sea, on and off, for a month or so, and had travelled less than four hundred miles up the coast. They had run out of flour and pork, with only a little rice left, and were trying to subsist on the fish they caught and on the small flying fish that from time to time landed in the boat. They dared not shoot seabirds, they had to conserve their precious powder. They were hungry, wet and chilly, and their boat was slowly sinking.

Every morning the cutter rode lower in the water, waves lapping along the boat's sides and sloshing over the sides every time the wind freshened. Not knowing what else to do, the convicts decided to throw their extra clothing overboard. Yet still the cutter sank lower, inch by inch, and nothing short of another overhaul and thorough caulking could prevent her from being swamped.

Will became disheartened, but Mary encouraged him— and the others. Her determination helped to rally the group, so that they had the nerve to attempt a risky landing.

"We ran into an open bay and could see no place to land," Martin wrote in his memoir of the voyage. A high and forceful surf was pounding at the shore, a churning surf so powerful that the convicts were afraid it would break their boat to bits. They anchored in the bay despite the dangerous surf, dropping the grapnel to weigh them down and prevent the cutter from being dragged under. But at about two o'clock in the morning, Martin recalled, "our grapling broke and we were drove in the middle of the surf expecting every moment that our boat would be staved to pieces and every soul perish."[3]

Flung up and under again and again by the pounding waves, the cutter ultimately, miraculously, floated free. No one aboard was thrown into the water. No one drowned. All were safe—albeit badly shaken. They had been at peril of drowning, gasping for breath as they were plunged repeatedly under thunderous breakers, in near total darkness, helpless against the walls of water that crashed over and about them in a frenzy of foam and spume.

But they had survived.

"As God would have it," wrote Martin, "we got our boat safe on shore without any damage excepting one oar. We hauled our boat up and there remained two days and two nights. There we kindled a fire with great difficulty, everything that we had being very wet."[4]

What name the convicts gave to this bay—Dangerous Cove or some similar formulation—is unknown. But they found shellfish there in abundance, and feasted on it, and did their best to dry themselves and their remaining possessions. There was no more rosin or beeswax; they had to coat the cutter's seams with soap, which proved to be effective against leaks. And as if in a final gift from a watchful providence, they were spared attack by the local tribes.

"The natives came down in great numbers," according to Martin. "We discharged a musket over their heads and they dispersed immediately, and we saw no more of them. We put our things in the boat and with great difficulty we got out to sea."[5]

They had no sooner got out to sea than a storm burst upon them, high winds lifting the seas into a roiling, menacing chop that made the cutter rock violently from side to side as rain pelted down out of angry dark clouds. They fought to hold on as the boat slid into black troughs and then rode high peaks of water, sheets of spray everywhere and the constant roar of the fierce wind loud in their ears.

The wind chopped from one corner of the sky to another, making for a rough and confused sea. Huge waves collided with one another, their crests tossing and breaking. The convicts took turns at the tiller, fighting to hold the laboring cutter steady into the oncoming waves, praying that she would not heel over in a gust or splinter under the force of a breaking wave.

Hour after frightening hour they held on, until their

hands and arms were stiff and sore from gripping the ropes and thwarts. Mary must have tied the children to herself or to the boat, otherwise they would have been swept overboard. All were wet to the skin with salt spray, drenched repeatedly as they bailed frantically in an effort to keep the cutter from being swamped. Fatigue overtook them, but they dared not sleep lest they drown. Without sleep, without food, they kept doggedly at the work of survival, steering, bailing, praying, enduring, their attempts at shouted communication lost amid the eerie howling of the wind. In the torrents of rain they could barely see—and when night fell, and the gale did not abate, they fought on in the blackness, clouds obscuring the moon, caught in a dim maelstrom of wind, rain and water that seemed to have no end.

For three days the powerful storm drove the fragile cutter and its eleven exhausted occupants before it, threatening to engulf them. When at last the wind began to die down and the sea to resume its familiar swell, they slept, too tired to eat, wet and sore and bone-weary.

The calm after the storm brought peace, but not comfort. Apart from the pain of physical exhaustion, and the pangs of hunger (for they had only a little rice left to eat), they were all suffering from saltwater sores, ulcers on the flesh, their pasty skins shrivelled and their lungs infected from inhaling too much salt spray. They coughed and wheezed, the children crying piteously, unable to understand why they had to endure such extreme discomfort.

Driven far offshore by the gale, the convicts found themselves in the open sea, out of sight of land. Guided by the sun, they attempted to sail and row toward where they thought the coast would be, watching for gannets and other shore birds and for the lightening and murkiness in the color of the water that would indicate that they were entering the shallows.

For days they watched the horizon, staring out into the infinity of blue water until their eyes were weary with the strain, but they glimpsed no land. Parched and famished, the men began to despair. They would die somewhere in the vast wilderness of ocean. When the last of the rice was gone, and they lacked the strength to try to fish, they would die of hunger—or of thirst.

"I will leave you to consider what distress we must be in," wrote James Martin, recalling the low spirits all the convicts felt after the gale, "the woman and the two little babies was in a bad condition, everything being so wet that we could by no means light a fire."[6] They had seen no land for eight days; on the ninth day, at eight in the morning, they sighted a small island and made landfall.

It was a very small island, about ninety miles offshore, but it seemed inaccessible, "the surf running so very high," Martin wrote, "that we were rather fearful of going in for fear of staving our boat." The nine starving convicts talked over what they should do, and at length came to a risky decision.

"We concluded amongst ourselves that we might as well venture in there as to keep out to sea, seeing no probability that if we kept out to sea we should every soul perish."[7]

They braved the fearsome surf, got through it without much damage to the boat and with no one drowned or lost, and hauled the cutter up onto the sandy beach. When they had made a fire and warmed themselves, and cooked the last grains of their rice, they set off, at low tide, to look for shellfish.

On the exposed reef they found a great many large turtles, and immediately took one and slaughtered it and "had a noble meal." It rained that night—a welcome rain, as there was no freshwater on the tiny island—and they spread the cutter's sail and filled their beakers with rainwater.

Secure on their own small island world, with turtles to feast on and in no fear of attack, the escapees rested and tried to recover their strength. For six days they ate their fill, slept, and ate their fill again, making up for many weeks of deprivation. They slaughtered more turtles and dried the meat to take with them on the next stage of their journey. For there was still a very long way to go—they had only reached twenty-six degrees latitude, by Will Morton's reckoning, only a third of the way to the nearest island in the Indonesian archipelago— the nearest Dutch settlement, the island of Timor.

But the going promised to be easier for the next thousand miles. For they had entered the Great Barrier Reef, the long coastal plateau of shallows sprinkled with hundreds of small islands. Captain Detmer Smith and the English sailors aboard the *Supply* must have told Will Bryant about the long expanse of reef, a hazard for sailing vessels but a haven for a small boat the size of the cutter. Here the projecting coral formed a protective barrier, shielding small craft from the wild waters of the open sea. The island offered coconuts and berries, shellfish and turtles. And the fish that swarmed in the coral shallows were abundant and easy to catch. Balmy air was said to prevail in the reef in autumn, a warm, sweet air that carried the scent of leafy trees and flowers.

After great hardship, they had arrived in a sort of paradise, where they could sail in security on the next leg of their voyage to freedom.[8] They stocked the cutter with dried turtle meat and a bellpepper-like fruit found on the island "which seemed to taste very well," wrote Martin.

"We could not think of taking any live turtles with us because our boat would not admit of it," he added. "We paid the seams of our boat all over with soap before we put to sea at eight o'clock in the morning and steered to the northward."

The next phase of the journey had begun.

XV

ITH A FRESH WIND at her back the cutter sailed, amid fair weather, across a fathomless turquoise sea, the water so clear that the voyagers could see far down into its depths. Dense forests of coral, some treelike and branching, some mushroomlike and round, spread out beneath them in gaudy colors of pink and yellow and red and brilliant blue. Blue butterfly fish, black and white angelfish and parrotfish in all colors of the rainbow swam in and out of the coral forests, dark grey eels with gold eyes and blue mouths emerged from crevices to gape, open-mouthed, at the spectacle around them. Fanlike green seaweed waved to and fro in the gentle currents. Through this slow-moving, dreamlike world drifted lionfish and grouper, sharks and jellyfish—a mysterious and mesmerizing procession of beautiful, poisonous creatures living in the warm, shallow waters of protected lagoons.

Herons and terns flew above the lagoons, and spotted crabs walked along their shores, parrots screeched in the island trees, while insects of many varieties buzzed through the air, landing on Mary and Will and the others and causing them to slap at their arms and legs and scratch where they were bitten. At night, when the turquoise water deepened to ultramarine blue and a tropical moon rose to shine on the glistening white sand, the muttonbird began its raucous crying, a rasping, grating screech far harsher than the call of a parrot.

The travellers might have been bewitched by the beauty around them, had they not been so hungry. For they soon consumed all the dried turtle meat they had brought with them, and could not find any more turtles to feast on. Nor could they catch enough of the abundant fish in the lagoons to keep themselves alive. They found crabs and shellfish in large quantities, but "none of them very fit to eat," Martin wrote. "But being very hungered we were glad to eat them and thank God for it. If it were not for the shellfish and the little turtle [meat] that we had we must have starved."[1]

Thin and weathered, weary of the long weeks of travelling, the convicts came at length to the Gulf of Carpentaria, a long stretch of open water with no protecting reef and swept by the monsoon wind from the north. They started southward down the coast of the gulf, only to encounter aboriginal people of a kind they had not met before. Stout, corpulent, ink-black and very warlike, these tribesmen, far from scattering when the convicts fired a musket round over their heads, fired back—with bows and arrows, which the aboriginals in more southerly latitudes had lacked. One of the arrows, lethal and very sharp and eighteen inches long, struck the cutter, but no one was harmed.

Escaping this attack, the convicts went on southward,

but two days later, as they were rowing in toward shore to fill their water beakers, they met with a terrifying sight.

Two large, long fighting canoes, each carrying thirty or forty aboriginal warriors, bore down on them rapidly, powered by paddles and sails woven from plant fronds. On a raised platform stood the warriors, weapons ready, led by their chief. Within moments the two canoes were joined by others.

"We did not know what to do," Martin recalled later, "for we were afraid to meet them." But there was no time for discussion. The cutter turned and made for the deep waters of the gulf, with the war canoes in rapid pursuit.

"They followed us until we lost sight of them. [We] determined to cross the gulf which was about five hundred miles across. As luck would have it, we outran them."[2]

They outran the war canoes—for the time being—but were now far out of sight of land, with very little fresh water and only a sketchy chart to guide them. In his laconic account of the voyage, James Martin says nothing about the state of the voyagers' spirits, whether they had become short-tempered and testy with one another—or even violent—after so many weeks living cheek by jowl in cramped quarters, whether they argued about what they should do or where they should go, whether Will and Mary were at odds, though they had been before. Now, setting off to cross the five hundred miles of the gulf with no islands to offer shellfish or water, and with every likelihood of encountering more of the frightening war canoes, the convicts must have been under very great strain.

For Mary, among the rough men, all of them shaggy-haired, bearded and stinking from nearly two months at sea, the task of enduring from day to day must have been monumental. Keeping the children alive took most of her strength and more than mere strength, for she had to feed Emanuel and she must have had little milk to give him. She had been "poorly," according to Martin, for weeks, the children peaked and lethargic. One hopes and imagines that the men were chivalrous and charitable to Mary and the children, but they too were focussed on their own survival.

All must have reacted in character to the venture they now undertook, the crossing of the wide gulf virtually without food or water: Mary with stoic endurance and rock-stubborn courage, Will capable but mercurial and hot-tempered, his energies running in fits and starts, James Martin observant, practical, analytical, Sam Bird the cunning Londoner doing his part, though he was weakening, blustering through.

Will Morton scanned his chart, watching for any indication that they might be off course, Nate Lilley pulled faithfully at his oar. The senior men, toughest of all, were stalwart, William Allen the experienced seaman, holding the tiller steady amid the strong swells, and tall, strong John Butcher the Worcestershire farmer, his ruddy face wind-roughened, lending his coarse-fibred vitality and sheer physical resilience.

It was the Second Fleeters Will Morton, Nate Lilley, Will Allen and John Butcher, one imagines, who anchored the crew psychologically. They had been through so much, living for months chained together in the dark holds of the transport ships, with water up to their waists, starved, beaten, shackled to dead men. Having lived through months of hell they were far tougher than any men, anywhere, had any right to be, their strength of will unrivalled.

In truth, however, much about the long voyage of Mary and Will and their companions is undiscoverable, because of the opacity of the sources. It may well be that by the time the travellers reached the Gulf of Carpentaria, some in the party were ill, perhaps too ill to row or bail, lying like dead weight in the bottom of the boat and a source of worry and strain to the others. Some may have begun to wander in their wits, to hallucinate or become hysterical as a result of malnutrition and severe thirst. All were gravely overtired, their equanimity and even their sanity under assault. It is significant that in James Martin's account of the voyage, he is all but silent about the final few weeks—which may have passed for him, as for the others, in a blur of pain and cravings and disconnected sensations.

Merely to go on: that was the challenge for them all. To set and sustain their course, bail out the water when the sea rushed in, stay as dry as they could, not fight over what remained of food and water. And keep, in the deepest part of their psyches, a steady flame of hope.

On the fifth day of open water travel across the wide gulf, the cutter came within reach of the western shore, and searched in vain for freshwater. Then, hardly pausing, the voyagers decided to go straight on across the Arafura Sea toward the island of Timor, easternmost of the Indonesian islands under Dutch rule. Their destination was the settlement of Kupang, which they knew of from Captain Smith. Once they reached Kupang they could find water and food, and then get on with the task of finding a way to disguise their identities and make new lives.

The wind was with them as they made their way swiftly across the emptiness of the Arafura Sea. They were parched and blistered from the sun, stiff and sore and longing for a respite from the punishments and discomforts of the voyage, but they knew that they were in the last stages of their long journey, and the knowledge must have helped them hang on through the last few days. It had been decided among them what they would say when they met the Dutch authorities, how they would account for themselves. They would say that they were survivors from the wreck of a whaling ship that sank or went aground. Will would introduce himself as the first mate of the ship, travelling with his wife and children. The others would pose as seamen. They must have colluded in inventing an elaborate story, giving a name to the invented whaler and deciding precisely when and where she foundered, who her captain was, what her tonnage and where her home port. None of the men, except possibly Will Allen, knew anything about whaling; they must have hoped that none of the Dutch at Kupang did either, and that they would not be closely questioned.

It was the strong, spicy scent of cloves in the air that told the travellers they were nearing their destination. That, and the increasing heat and humidity. Soon the indistinct outline of land came into view, its mountain peaks rising as if out of the sea. They followed along the southern coast of the island, passing promontory after green promontory, the entire place a lush, green Eden where tropical forests adjoined acre after acre of carefully manicured cultivated land. Soon the perfume of ginger and frangipani mingled with the fragrance of clove to produce a powerful, heady scent. They rounded the western end of the island and glimpsed a fortress, built on high stone ramparts and surrounded on the lower slopes by houses set in flowering gardens. A crowd gathered as the cutter approached the wharf. After sixty-nine days and nearly thirty-three hundred miles, the long fatiguing journey was finally over. They had safely reached Kupang.

The strangers who got out of the small boat, helped by hospitable, sympathetic Malays and Dutch colonists who rushed forward to greet them, were unwashed and bedraggled. Their clothing was torn, their skin red and scorched by exposure to the tropical sun and covered with blisters and sores. Hollow-eyed, unsteady on their feet, stinking of sweat and encrusted with salt, the eleven passengers stepped out onto the wharf, reduced to tears by the first kind welcome they had experienced in ten weeks.

Food and water were offered them, and they ate and drank greedily, only to have their bodies reject what they had so eagerly consumed. It was days before they could keep anything down but tea and milk, weeks before their sunburned, ulcerated bodies began to heal. In the meantime the governor of Timor, Timotheus Wanjon, treated them as honored guests. "He behaved extremely well to us," wrote Martin, "filled our bellies and clothed [us] double with every [thing] that was worn on the island." Mary was wrapped in a sarong, the men too given sarongs and embroidered tunics. Emanuel was swathed in a length of batik cloth, and Charlotte given a smock of the kind the Malayan children wore—when they wore anything at all.

The visitors told Governor Wanjon and his staff their story of shipwreck and survival, and were much admired and praised. Mary was particularly singled out for her strength and courage in enduring the hardships of the open sea and protecting her children. Evidently the convicts were believed; Captain Smith, the only person who could have contradicted their story, was not present to betray them, and no one else had any idea who they really were. They were British, and the Dutch knew that the British had a penal colony in New Holland, thousands of miles to the south. But it would not have occurred to anyone in Kupang that a group of convicts from Port Jackson could sail a small boat all the way to Timor; that would have been unthinkable. To be sure, the English Captain Bligh had made a thirty-five-hundred-mile sea journey in an open longboat, and had landed on Timor only two years earlier. But Captain Bligh was an experienced naval officer, and these poor starveling wretches were civilians, ordinary seamen and a seaman's wife and children. That they might have accomplished a feat equal to Bligh's was beyond imagination.

So began, for Mary, the most peaceful and idyllic season of her adult life. Each day she ate her fill, each night she slept on clean sheets in a soft bed provided by Governor Wanjon. There were no shackles, no guards, no regulations, no rough taunts and jibes—only a delicious freedom, approving glances, empathetic people to nurse her back to health and to offer her whatever she needed. To find herself surrounded by warmth and solicitude, after so many years of coldness and punitive deprivation, must have made Mary's tears flow daily. Harshness gave way to softness, rigor to relaxation and ease. Gradually, as she put on weight and her raw skin began to heal, Mary must have felt her muscles unclench and her nerves cease to be locked in constant vigilance.

Everything about Kupang, even the relentless ninety-degree heat and near hundred-percent humidity of the dry season, invited Mary to indulge her senses and take her pleasure. A profusion of orchids and sweet-scented shrubs lined her paths. A cooling breeze from the ocean swept over her as she sat on the wide verandah in the evening. Enticing music, unlike any she had ever heard, a metallic chiming and clanging of gongs and keys, drifted through the city from dozens of gamelan orchestras playing in mansions and squares and public buildings. To eat she had sticky rice sweets wrapped in banana leaves and filled with the juice of brown sugar, skewers of spicy roast meet, mangos and papayas, red rambutan and greenish durian and purple mangosteen. Cold beer made the food go down well, and there was always coconut juice and sweet coconut flesh in abundance.

Of course, Mary had to be careful about what she ate, and about what she gave Charlotte to eat. Some of the fruit in the marketplace was unclean, and she was cautioned that eating it could bring on severe diarrhea, dehydration and death. There were fevers in Timor; the surgeons at the town hospital dispensed "bark of Peru" (chinchona bark, or quinine) mixed with wine to counteract them. When Mary strolled through the marketplace she saw the "Jamu ladies" who sold an array of traditional herbal medicines to treat fevers and colds—indeed, to treat everything from sore throats to infected teeth to impotence.

A variety of exotic goods, offered by an ethnically diverse group of traders, filled the marketplace. For Kupang, small though it was, was a major trading center and ships from all over Asia and the Pacific, Africa and Europe called there. To wander past its crowded stalls was to encounter fragrant sandalwood, spicy padang food, mounds of rice and lengths of colorful batik cloth. There were shadow puppets and carved wooden door frames, intricate silver jewelry, opium scales and blowguns and brassware from India.

Five times throughout the day the call to prayer was heard floating over the rooftops, for Timor was overwhelmingly Muslim in population and on Fridays, men and boys in bright sarongs and tightly fitting black caps gathered at the mosques for prayers.

The strangeness of it all, the oppressive heat and lavish color, the sheer prodigality of life in the tropics must have given Mary much to ponder as she recovered her strength and thought about her situation. With the others, she had taken her freedom, made good her escape. Against high odds, she and her children had been spared death or disaster.

But where was she to go from here? What sort of future was she to have?

The men found work in Kupang, and settled in.[3] No doubt they used aliases—Will took Mary's maiden name and called himself "William Broad"—and continued to maintain the deception that they were honest seamen who had survived shipwreck. But by staying in Kupang instead of moving on, looking for berths on outgoing ships or resettling in even more remote locations, the convicts were taking a considerable risk. And they seem to have been shortsighted in exposing themselves to that risk.

As long as they remained in Kupang, they were bound together by their common secret. The safety of each of them depended on the loyalty and silence of the others. But Will, ever restless and ambitious, was discontented, and could not find a comfortable life amid the flowering gardens and clove-scented wharves of the Dutch settlement.

What happened was most likely very simple: Will wanted his independence.

He had never considered his marriage to Mary to be legal; what emotional ties there were between them seem to have frayed past any possibility of repair. Any love he felt for his small son and stepdaughter may only have made him conflicted—and irritable. Possibly he acquired a mistress in Kupang, causing a rift with Mary. Or possibly it was Mary who was wayward, or perhaps she hounded him past endurance about what she perceived as his inadequacies, or about his obligations to her and the children. What is certain is that a growing hostility developed between them—a hostility that was to lead, over the next several months, to their downfall.

XVI

FOR SEVERAL MONTHS Mary and her fellow escapees continued to ingratiate themselves with their Dutch and Indonesian hosts and to perpetuate the myth that they were the fortunate survivors of a shipwreck. Once the men recovered their strength they found work, probably well-paying work on the busy wharf, and settled into the life of the small but cosmopolitan port. Kupang was thriving; no doubt the men hoped to thrive with it, and grow rich. If it occurred to them that in continuing to stay there they were risking exposure as impostors, with their true identities discovered, they took no action to protect themselves. Any or all of the men might have hired on as seamen on a merchant vessel, or booked an inexpensive passage to China or Cape Town or Calcutta as passengers. Instead they chose to stay, at least for awhile, in Kupang where the hot, tropical life was full of ease and pleasure, the wages were good and the local beer pungent and free-flowing.

Possibly they quarrelled among themselves, or old grievances began to fester beneath the pleasant surface. It could be that the nine escapees were planning yet another collective voyage, together, and the planning was marred by disagreements or stalemated by unexpected circumstances. Perhaps some wanted to stay in Kupang, others to move on before their luck ran out, and they could not reach a consensus.

Will was angry. In his view he had served his seven-year sentence, and deserved his freedom. Had he stayed in Sydney Cove, the authorities would have forced him to remain in the settlement for many years to support his wife and son and stepdaughter. But he was not under that constraint in Kupang. Once he left the penal settlement, Will reasoned, he was not even legally married any longer. But as long as he stayed in Kupang, he had to maintain the fiction that he was "Will Broad," as he called himself, family man and first mate of an imaginary whaling ship. He had to stay with Mary, or the entire story would begin to unravel.

But he chafed, or Mary goaded him, until he lost patience. And in his fit of temper, Will betrayed them all.

According to James Martin, "William Bryant had words with his wife and informed against himself, wife and children and all of us."[1]

Whether he let the truth out in a drunken rage in a wharfside tavern, or tried to buy his own free passage out of Kupang by bargaining with the Dutch governor or one of his deputies, or whether he simply broke down and blurted out the truth in a moment of weakness, Will's admission sealed his own fate and that of his comrades.

"We was immediately taken prisoners and was put into the castle," Martin wrote. Having been deceived by the convicts for two months, the Dutch now showed them no leniency.

All nine adults and the two children were shackled and confined, all their comforts denied them. According to one account, Mary tried to run into the jungle with her children and hide from the Dutch soldiers, only to be captured like the others and deprived of her liberty.

It would have been in character for her to make a desperate dash for freedom, and in keeping with the state in which she now found herself. For Will, though still her husband, had abandoned her and the children, just as he had abandoned his comrades. With a few malicious words he had ensured that all the adults in the escape party would not only be imprisoned once again, but would be condemned to death. Escaped prisoners in Port Jackson, once recaptured, were executed; the convicts could expect nothing less. The Dutch would turn them all over to the British, who would see to it that they all were hanged.

Mary tried to flee, but failed. She was taken, bound, and shut away in the dark and stench of the castle dungeon, with her hapless children. All of the pleasures and delights of the past several months, the abundant food and soft bed, the approval and hospitality, the warm flower-scented breezes, were suddenly snatched away—along with any chance at a future. The open door of freedom was slammed shut. And all because of Will.

Mary's chagrin, mortification and sheer rage must have been monumental. After all that she had risked, after all that she had endured, the months at sea, the hunger and thirst, the storms and huge waves, the sores and blisters and illness: after all that, to be handed over to new captors by the man she depended on most. She had fought with Will; now she must have wanted to murder him.

Governor Wanjon now had eleven prisoners on his hands. He needed to deliver them to the nearest British authorities, but it might be many months before a British ship called at Kupang. How was he to discharge his obligation?

A solution presented itself, far more quickly than he suspected. The escapees were imprisoned in the castle sometime in August of 1791. In mid-September, four small boats entered Kupang Harbor, filled with British sailors. They were the survivors of the *Pandora*, wrecked on a reef in the coral seas. Among them was the *Pandora*'s captain, Edward Edwards, and it was to Edwards that Governor Wanjon now delivered his prisoners.[2]

Edwards was a stern, hard man, a man who subjected those under him to a punishing severity and gave no quarter. He had been prized for his severity, in fact, by the British Admiralty and had been given command of the *Pandora* because it was felt that he would carry out an unusual mission with exceptional efficiency.

Captain Edwards and his crew had been sent from England in search of the mutinous crew members of William Bligh's ship *Bounty*. After a difficult voyage during which many in the crew had come down with fever, Edwards managed to recapture fourteen of the *Bounty*'s mutineers, who had settled in Tahiti. (The remnant of the mutinous crew members, who had gone to Pitcairn Island, eluded him.)

As his Admiralty superiors had foreseen, Edwards showed the mutinous sailors no mercy. They were shackled, their legs and hands bound together, and kept in a specially built prison cell on the *Pandora*'s deck. No contact between the prisoners and the crew of the *Pandora* was allowed, and the sufferings of the men, crammed together in their filth-ridden small cell, were an offense to the others on board. To all the others, that is, except Captain Edwards, who thought the treatment appropriate for sailors who had set their own captain adrift to die, and taken over his ship.

Then the *Pandora* herself became imperilled. On the westward journey to Timor Edwards, as demanding of the sea as he was of his men, and refusing to make allowances for the hazardous reefs of the Torres Strait, sailed his ship across a stretch of dangerous water at night. The decision was foolhardy in the extreme; the ship was driven onto a reef and wrecked.

The panicked crew bailed all night, but could not prevent the ship from foundering. As it went down, the prisoners cried for help. Common humanity demanded that they be released from their shackles to prevent them from drowning. They were not, after all, convicted criminals but accused prisoners awaiting trial. But Edwards refused to release them, and left them to their fate while he himself swam to safety.

The mutineers would all have drowned, had not the bosun's mate rescued them from their confining cell and removed their heavy iron shackles. Even so, and despite the bosun's heroism, four of the men drowned. (Edwards was subsequently court-martialled, but that was far in the future.)

Fresh from the extreme trauma of shipwreck, having lost his vessel and recovered only some of the mutineers he had been sent to capture, Edwards was still doggedly duty-bound. Far from chastening or softening him, trauma only hardened him further, and made him severe in his treatment of the British convicts Governor Wanjon turned over to him. Edwards hired a Dutch transport ship, the *Rembang*, to take his crew and prisoners to Batavia, where he expected to be able to find a British ship for the return journey to England.

And he made certain that for all his captives, the voyage aboard the *Rembang* would be one of stark privation and harsh discipline.

In chains, her children and few possessions with her, Mary went aboard the *Rembang* in the first week of October, 1791. The ship reeked of cloves, its usual cargo, and of stale cooking and human sweat and ordure—a cloying reek that she recalled immediately from the *Dunkirk* and the *Charlotte*. But aboard the prison hulk and the British transport ship she had at least been free to move, and to wash herself and Charlotte, after a fashion, to go on deck occasionally. Through portholes and chinks in the planking she had been able to watch the changing light in the sky and the pattern of clouds and rain, the dark squalls marching across the horizon and, during rough weather, the green swells of heavy seas and tall combers, approaching rank on rank.

On the small *Rembang*, however, the guards shut her in an airless, lightless enclosure with her fellow convicts, and fastened a heavy iron shackle to her ankles, making it very difficult to move, as the shackle was fastened to a long iron bar attached to the flooring. She was more tightly imprisoned than ever before, her ankles soon raw from the scraping of the irons, her leg and back muscles aching, all her senses quickened in the dimness, her eyes longing for the light. Even the smallest and most needful tasks, such as relieving herself in the common bucket, took great effort. She had no way to wash herself or the children—Captain Edwards had forbidden the convicts any water for washing—and could not prevent the lice that crawled over her from making her skin itch unbearably or the rats that snatched at her food from nipping at the children.

Worst of all, shackled as she was, Mary knew that,

should the *Rembang* founder in a storm, she and the children would surely drown, weighed down as they were and fastened to the thick planks. And Captain Edwards had already driven one ship to destruction, causing many deaths. He might well cause this ship too to wreck itself on some dangerous reef, or capsize in rough weather. Added to her rage at Will and her fear of the death by execution that awaited her once she reached far-off England was the more immediate fear of drowning in the warm tropical ocean, with its sharks and fearsome eels and stinging jellyfish, on the voyage to Batavia in the coming weeks.

She had no idea how far it was to Batavia of course, or what would happen to her once she got there. For all she knew there would be a long delay before the ship sailed, or, just possibly, a form of reprieve. She had been reprieved once, after all, five and a half years earlier when she had been in Exeter jail awaiting execution. Was it just barely conceivable that another official, finding her to be more useful alive than dead, might send her to another penal colony in lieu of returning her to England?

Sanguine as she was, such thoughts may have drifted at the edge of Mary's consciousness, as much wish or prayer as actual conjecture. Envisioning freedom may have helped to keep her mind from harsher thoughts: the clove-laden stench of the common cell, the appeals of her incomprehending son and daughter, the hateful presence of Will, the discomfiting nearness of the other men, her constant hunger and thirst.

Once the *Rembang* got under way, however, it was hard to find any distraction, mental or otherwise, from the lurching of the pitching, rolling ship. With every shift in the vessel's horizontal, the convicts' ankle shackles slid along the metal bar, jamming Mary and the children up against the men, with bruising force. So yanked and thrust about, it was nearly impossible to sleep or eat, and at times even breathing was a struggle against the contrary force of the waves and wind.

As had been true during Mary's long voyage from Sydney to Timor, she had to live hour by hour alongside men, with no privacy—not when she nursed Emanuel, not when she attended to her menstrual needs, not when she was seasick or suffering from cramps or bowel complaints.

And suffering there must have been, general suffering, in the dimness of the foul-smelling chamber, where with the merciless rocking of the ship the convicts must have vomited over one another and lived in the reek of one another's noxious effluvia. With little light and no fresh air, scant food and water, no exercise and no relief from their common misery—for Captain Edwards had ordered that the convicts never be allowed to go on deck or have their shackles loosened—the prisoners soon became thin and despondent. When the *Rembang* sailed into the path of a destructive hurricane, their despondency gave way to sheer terror.

It was the most violent, most spectacular storm the English officers had ever seen. Sudden brilliant flashes of lightning split the sky with a crack and thunder, with a roar as of a thousand cannon, boomed a fearsome reply.

"This storm," wrote the overawed Surgeon Hamilton, lately of the *Pandora*, "was attended with the most dreadful thunder and lightning we had ever experienced." The cyclonic wind tore the sails of the *Rembang* to shreds before the sailors could take them in, while high seas, churned to boiling froth, swept over the *Rembang*'s deck in wave after pounding wave until the ship sprang a leak. Pumps could make no headway against such a torrent of angry water; they soon became clogged, and in the hold, the bilge rose, threatening to flood the deck where the convicts and the *Bounty* mutineers were confined.

Pitched crazily from side to side, wet through from all the flooding, unable to see the storm but hearing the loud boom of the thunder and the whiplike crack of each bolt of lightning, Mary and the others knew the fear of imminent death. They yelled to the *Rembang* crew, begging to be released from their shackles and let out of their cell. They cursed and swore, they damned Will to hell—as they had often done before—and when no one came in response to their pleas, they used all their strength to try to get free of the thick irons by smashing them against one another and pulling and straining.

It was futile. The old shackles held firm. The iron bar could not be torn out of the floor. The Dutch crew, who according to Surgeon Hamilton were "struck with horror" and hid belowdecks, ignored the convicts' yells and pleas. And the British sailors, having survived the sinking of the *Pandora* and desperate to save themselves and the *Rembang* from a similar fate, were fully engaged in trying to prevent the ship from being driven against the shore of nearby Flores Island.

"She was driving down, with all the impetuosity imaginable, on a savage shore, about seven miles under our lee," wrote Hamilton. But though the "abyss of destruction" yawned before them all, and every force of nature seemed to conspire against them, the "manly exertions" of the sailors were in the end effectual. The *Rembang* was steered clear of the dangerous coast, her bilges were pumped and the flooding slowed, her leak patched and eventually, after many hours of being tossed in the massive chaotic waves, the storm died down.

Mary and the others were wet, feverish, exhausted and shaken. But they were alive.

They were alive—yet weakened, and becoming ill. By the second or third week of the voyage, many in the crew and among the passengers had fevers, and were listless and glassy-eyed, their appetites gone and their muscles lax and sore. Mary may have been feverish herself. Her baby certainly was, little Emanuel, now a year and a half old, able to walk and talk but subdued by the trauma he had been through and by the disease that had invaded his small body. He cried in his suffering, and Mary did what little she could to offer him comfort, as the *Rembang*, with new sails in place, ran on along the islands of the Bali Sea toward Java.

A burning, scorching sun shone down on the Dutch ship after the storm passed. It was November, near the height of the equatorial summer, and the vessel floated on a warm sea blanketed in thick moist air. The convicts were parched, but Captain Edwards had strictly limited their supply of water, with no exceptions made for those who had come down with the fever. Surgeon Hamilton may have examined those of the convicts who were ill, including baby Emanuel, and if he did, most likely he recognized the onset of malaria, and knew that there was little he could do to counteract it. Infants were particularly susceptible, and suffered more acutely than adults from what was called "brain fever" because of the delirium it caused.

As for Mary, debilitated herself and longing for relief from the heat, she held her son and tried to nurse him— though she probably had no milk to give him—and did her best to comfort Charlotte through the last trying days before the *Rembang* reached Batavia and dropped anchor in the wide harbor, the sea flecked with a million sparkling points of light under the fiercely shining sun.

XVII

*H*EAT, HIGH HUMIDITY and fatal malarial fevers were the things Batavia was known for. The Dutch colonizers had been there for two centuries, giving their fortresslike settlement the new name Batavia in preference to the traditional Javanese name of Jacatra, and making it look as much like a Dutch town as possible, with multistory brick houses and tall-steepled churches and long, straight canals like the canals of Amsterdam. Except in the sprawling Chinese quarter, where the potent liquor called arrack was brewed and much lucrative traffic in trade goods went on, Batavia was a town of Dutchmen, Dutchmen who drank heavily and smoked their outsize white meerschaum pipes and enjoyed themselves all the more lustily for knowing they were stalked by the deadly fever and that most of them would not survive for long.

Captain Edwards, wanting to prevent the further spread of malaria among his crew, ordered all those aboard the *Rembang* who were ill to be rowed ashore and taken to the hospital. Emanuel was among those sent ashore, pale and weak, his skin hot to the touch. Mary held him in her arms as the *Rembang*'s longboat was rowed across the harbor and into one of the town canals. A putrid odor rose from the stagnant canal water on which floated garbage—and worse. According to Surgeon Hamilton, who was accompanying the sick to the hospital, "some dead bodies floating down a canal struck our boat, which had a very disagreeable effect on the minds of our brave fellows, whose nerves were reduced to a very weak state from sickness."

The ghoulish collision with the corpses must have had a horripilating effect on Mary as well, who may have been as ill as her son and imagining that she might die in Batavia. In the filthy, mosquito-ridden hospital, centuries old and in a deplorable state of decay, it was as if the sick, injured and dying were forgotten and abandoned. Few of those who entered the hospital were cured; they died swiftly, or wasted slowly in their suffering, until their bodies were removed and thrown into the canal to make room for more victims.

Whether she lay, neglected and fever-ridden, on the dirty floor of the dank old building, full of the reek of massed unwashed humanity, or sat with her weakening baby, well enough to be in anguish over his condition, Mary must have been in great agony of spirit over the following several weeks. The wretchedness of her dear son, crying almost continuously, unable to rest or eat, the disease invading his brain until he writhed and moaned in his delirium, was surely heartrending. And the impact of his suffering was only underscored by the presence of so many others, carried in or brought in on pallets by the score each day, all of them groaning and crying or shrieking in delirium in a dismal chorus of pain and futile complaint.

The heat grew worse, a heavy muggy heat that drained Mary of energy and made the hours pass in an oppressive haze of thirst and sweat and discomfort. Mosquitoes rose in clouds from the still, odorous waters of the canals. Flies crawled over the carrion, lizards slithered up and down the hospital walls, their tongues darting out to catch the insects that buzzed and whirred and clustered on every available surface. Death was everywhere, in the oppressive heat, almost unbearable at midday, that caused Mary to feel faint, in the animals devouring and being devoured, grinning from the corpses, their limbs stiffly extended, their eyes staring, their mouths set in a smiling rictus.

And in Emanuel's white small face, as he grew ever more shrunken and skeletal until he became too weak to cry or even to lift his thin arms. He passed from life on December 1, 1791, three weeks after the *Rembang* landed in Batavia, and was buried in haste in a cemetery that already held far too many graves, and his mother mourned him.

Six days later Will Bryant caught the fever and was taken to the hospital, where after two weeks he too succumbed and died, and was taken to lie beside his son.

Mary, now transferred with Charlotte and the remaining convicts to a Dutch guard ship, must have been numb with fatigue and sorrow—and was ill herself. When by Captain Edwards' orders she and Charlotte were put aboard the Dutch ship *Horssen* for the journey from Batavia to Cape Town, the Dutch captain did not shackle her as ordered but let her retain her freedom of movement so that she could look after her four-year-old daughter.

For as the *Horssen* left Batavia and made its way through the Straits of Sunda toward the Indian Ocean, passengers

and crew were shivering and sweating with malaria. Nearly everyone was sick. One by one the men began dying, their bodies shrouded in lengths of linen and dropped over the side of the ship. Soon the surviving members of the crew were so ill it took a great effort on their part to rouse themselves sufficiently to rid the ship of the dead.

The *Horssen* sailed on, officers filling in where the crew was depleted, through muggy days and weeks, with water rationed to one quart per day per person. Mary and Charlotte did not die, but unknown to Mary, several of her companions in the escape from Port Jackson succumbed. Will Morton, navigator of the escape, and Sam Bird of Croydon, both of whom had been put aboard the Dutch ship *Hoornwey*, died on their voyage.[1] And Banbury Jack, ever the most daring of the escapees, escaped once again, by jumping overboard in the narrow Strait of Sunda and swimming toward shore.

The odds were against him; if the sharks didn't eat him, and the currents didn't carry him in the wrong direction, he would still have had to swim through the high surf near shore and risk being driven down into the razor-sharp coral by the pounding waves. And his hands were shackled, so that he could not swim properly. Unless, of course, he had found a way to overcome the odds, loosing himself from his fetters before he leaped into the water, timing his jump so that he avoided both unfavorable currents and high surf, and choosing a moment when the ship was very close to shore. No one knows for certain what happened to Banbury Jack. Maybe he made it to safety.

For three months the *Horssen* fought her way toward the Cape, the sailing rough and the weather hot, until on March 18, 1792, she landed at last in Table Bay. By good fortune there was a British ship in port, the *Gorgon*, and on board the *Gorgon* were men familiar to Mary and the remaining convicts who arrived on the *Hoornwey*.

The *Gorgon* had come from Port Jackson, where a number of marine officers, their wives and children had come aboard for the homeward journey to England.

"We was put on board the *Gorgon*," James Martin wrote in his memoir, "which we was known well [sic] by all the marine officers which was all glad that we had not perished at sea."[2] The surviving convicts, Mary and James Martin, Will Allen, Nate Lilley and John Butcher, reunited for the first time in three months, now discovered that to their former guards, the marine officers from Port Jackson, they were not pariahs but celebrities, heroes who had achieved an all but impossible feat of seamanship. Captain John Parker and his wife, Captain Watkin Tench and Lieutenant Ralph Clark were familiar faces, as were the few additional passengers on the *Gorgon*, officers' wives and children and ex-convicts whose terms had expired and who were going back to England as free men.

It must have been an odd sort of reunion for them all; on the one hand the marines and others were genuinely glad that at least five of the escapees, plus little Charlotte, had survived their bold journey to Timor, but on the other hand, everyone knew that the *Gorgon* would be taking Mary and the others back to England to be punished for their crime. Perhaps, privately, Parker, Tench and the others wished that their captives could be pardoned and freed. But in their official capacity they could not express such an opinion, they could only say how glad they were that the remnant of the escape party was still alive.

And they could exchange news with the convicts, hearing the details of their remarkable voyage, their time in Timor and Batavia, the misfortune (as it surely must have seemed) of their recapture. From the ex-convicts, the marines and their wives Mary must have learned of the arrival in Port Jackson of the Third Fleet, ten ships bringing more than eighteen hundred convicts, many of them with severe dysentery.

Slowly, despite the obstacles of illness and harsh weather and poor soil, the penal colony was growing. Yet everyone aboard the *Gorgon*, from Captain Parker to the youngest cabin boy, was relieved to be away from Sydney Cove, returning to England. Everyone, that is, but the *Bounty* mutineers and the five escape survivors. For them, the *Gorgon* voyage, and the few comforts it offered, was their last taste of relative freedom. Once the ship reached London, they would be imprisoned, to await trial and execution.

Meanwhile, however, they were well treated. The stern Captain Edwards, with his *Bounty* mutineers, was a louring presence on the *Gorgon* during the voyage, but he was no longer in command, he was merely one passenger among many. Captain Parker's greater humanity and leniency set the tone for the convicts' treatment, and he saw to it that Mary and Charlotte had decent accommodations and were adequately fed.

The *Gorgon* rounded the Cape and began her journey to the West African coast. "Very hot," Lieutenant Clark wrote in his journal. "At night, below the gun deck, there is hardly any living for the heat."

The ship's upper deck was crowded with live animals, kangaroos and wombats and koalas, lorikeets and galahs and screeching parrots. The animals were accustomed to high, desertlike heat; the human passengers were not, and once again, as on the *Horssen* and the *Rembang*, they began to get sick.

The children suffered most acutely. By the third week of

the *Gorgon*'s voyage several of the marines' sons and daughters had died, and others were weakening. It may have been an outbreak of malaria, or some other kind of deadly fever—West Africa was known as the "Fever Coast"—but the precise diagnosis mattered little. The ship's surgeon had no cure for the terrible chills and high temperature, the vomiting and diarrhea, the aching and lethargy that overtook the sufferers and in the end led to their complete physical collapse.

Bleeding them from a vein—the most common treatment for fever at that time—did no good. Cold baths might have helped but they were an impossibility on a sailing ship where there was no ice and the air temperature was far in excess of a hundred degrees. The children languished, watched over by anxious adults who were themselves debilitated by the effects of the unrelenting fierce heat and pitiless sun. Their supplies of fresh food were gone, they were eating salt pork and stale bread, washed down with water green with algae and teeming with wriggling larval life.

"The children are going very fast," Lieutenant Clark recorded in the fourth week of the voyage. "The hot weather is the reason for it."

On May 4, 1792, the sixth child to be buried at sea was wrapped in a cloth shroud and put over the side, the grieving parents standing helplessly by. The following day there was yet another small shroud, another hastily spoken prayer by the chaplain, another subdued splash as the seventh body sank into the warm ocean.

Charlotte, her face waxen and her wasted body hot to the touch, lay near death. Mary had done all she could for her, but the heat and fever were overpowering, and the child had not been strong enough to overcome them. At four and a half, Charlotte was old enough to comprehend what lay in store for her when the *Gorgon* reached England. Her mother would be taken to prison to die, and she herself would face an unknown future alone, in a land she had never seen. Her stepfather, the only father she had ever known, had died in Batavia, along with her baby brother. Soon she would lose her mother as well. Young as she was, Charlotte may well have given in to despair as the fever took over her small body. She may not have fought for life.

As Mary watched her daughter grow thinner and weaker, her pulse racing and her voice so faint it was only a whisper, she must have wept and grieved. She had kept Charlotte alive through so many ordeals, from her birth on shipboard through her early months of life during the rough and stormy passage to Port Jackson, through the hard days of near starvation in Sydney Cove, and then through the long perilous escape journey, and the rough passage from Timor to Batavia. At every stage of their life together, Mary had nurtured and protected her daughter, and Charlotte had proven to be, like Mary herself, a hardy survivor. Now all her hardihood had left her, she had surrendered to the disease that was conquering her frail body. Mary knew that she would not live.

Through the early predawn hours of May 6, 1792, it rained heavily off the coast of West Africa, squalls sweeping across the sky and the sea churning with frothy waves and foam. The rain brought a welcome cooling breeze that rattled the *Gorgon*'s hawsers and puffed out the sails, making it easier for the passengers to sleep and easing the muggy tedium of the night watch.

Charlotte lay on her cot, motionless save for the rising and falling of her narrow chest. Her eyes were closed, her limbs stiff and rigid. She struggled to breathe. The surgeon had come and gone. There was nothing to do now but wait.

And so Mary waited, sitting by her daughter's bedside, a

swinging candle lantern throwing waves of light across the cot as the ship rolled from side to side. It had been five years and more since she left England, a hardened young woman of twenty-two, for parts unknown. She had been carrying Charlotte then, as yet unborn, the unlooked-for result of her lovemaking with the long-vanished Mr. Spence. Did she think of him now, in the last hours before dawn, or did she ponder the curious synchrony between Charlotte's life, now approaching its end, and her own prolonged adventure?

It was dim; she was tired from her long vigil. As the ship's bell sounded the hours, Mary may have nodded off.

On the morning of May 6, Lieutenant Clark made another entry in his journal. "Last night the child belonging to Mary Broad, the convict woman who went away in the fishing boat from Port Jackson last year, died at about four o'clock. Committed body to the deep."

XVIII

THICK CLOUDS OF SMOKE and soot hung over the great sprawling metropolis of London in the spring of 1792, and a pall of dinginess seemed to over-spread everything, from the newly laid-out squares and freshly turned earth of market gardens to the north to the twisting alleys off the Strand to the proud new wings added to the Bank of England where the old church of St. Christopher-le-Stocks formerly stood. All was mud, murk and grey dullness, or so it seemed to a French visitor; unlike airy, buoyant, free-spirited Paris, London seemed to the Frenchman to stagger under a load of coal dust and grit, the outscourings of a thousand active building sites and ten thousand chimneys.

There was congestion everywhere, from the narrow streets crowded with pedestrians and wagons, carriages and flocks of sheep to the dim and crooked passageways of

Alsatia, where thieves and murderers, pickpockets and prostitutes found refuge, to the prosperous lanes of the commercial City and the noisy open-air markets whose stalls held cod and herring, sides of beef and mounds of cucumbers and tomatoes, apples and pears. Shouting, jostling carters muscled their way along, footmen and messengers bullied and elbowed past slower-moving traffic and in Covent Garden, alluring half-naked courtesans, their long hair loose and tumbled about their shoulders, called from the windows of the bathhouses to prospective customers in the street below.

The dirt, the noise and crowds, above all the rapid, ravenous growth of the capital as open fields and marshlands filled with new streets and squares gave London a savage impersonality. People, houses, entire neighborhoods were crushed and swept away in the relentless turmoil of expansion. The old, the weak, the powerless were ground under, left behind, forgotten. And while there were foundling homes for abandoned children and hospitals for the infirm, institutions for reformed streetwalkers and open-air Methodist revivals where tens of thousands were welcomed to abjure "the folly and madness of this sensible world," still most of London's lower classes were left to fend for themselves. Emigrants from the countryside, unable to find steady work in the city, huddled in doorways and cellars, homeless and dispirited; many were arrested and sent to Bridewell Prison as vagrants, the most hapless were found dead and carted off by the night watchmen, to be laid nameless in common graves.

The city's East End, with its ragged slums and reeking breweries and wharves, was worlds away from the grand squares and waterside mansions, the pleasure gardens and elegant shops of the fashionable West End. Here the chief concerns, among the conspicuously well-dressed and well-coiffed members of the privileged classes, were social and financial: the issuing and receiving of invitations to dinners and balls, the cultivation of powerful contacts, the making of advantageous marriages. In the small, tight-knit world of the West End, where the grinding clatter of carriage wheels on cobblestones marked the hours of visiting, shopping, appointments with tailors and dressmakers and dining out, money and property were of all-absorbing interest—and along with money and property, the social and political stability that assured their safety.

But in the spring of 1792, that stability was under assault. Rioters aggrieved over low wages and high food prices were kept under control with great difficulty by constables and watchmen and, under extreme conditions, by soldiers. Political agitators stirred angry passions and aroused inchoate but dangerous resentments. In the worst of the assaults, violent crowds broke windows and overturned fences, looted shops—especially London's ubiquitous gin shops—and vented their rage, as they had for centuries, by plundering the mansions of the well-to-do.

There was much talk, in that uneasy spring of 1792, of what was seen as the true source of all the trouble: the ever more radical revolution in France.

Since 1789 the French, especially the Parisians, had been dismantling their society and overturning the time-honored social order. The king, Louis XVI, was still on his throne but had been reduced to presiding over a constitutional monarchy, as a puppet of elected legislative bodies whose politics were moving farther and farther to the left. Class distinctions, hereditary titles and feudal rights had evaporated; all men were, in revolutionary theory, equal, and the motto "Liberty, Equality, Fraternity" was carved into monuments and printed on pamphlets and in newspapers until it became synonymous with the aims and ideals of the new constitutional government. By fiat all men were declared to be of equal rank, and in 1792 there was much talk of carrying this ideal of equality one step further, to include women.

In the salons of London's West End, *A Vindication of the Rights of Women*, Mary Wollstonecraft's feminist manifesto, was being widely read and discussed. Wollstonecraft herself was for the moment the most famous and most controversial woman in Europe (though she would soon be eclipsed by Charlotte Corday, the murderer of Jean-Paul Marat), and her claim that women should be given equal political rights with men was one inflammatory idea among many in what was being called "the woman question."

There was no end, it seemed, to the dangerously corrupting notions incubating in France and infecting the English populace. The French had abolished the church and worshipped Reason, removing the sanction of religion as a buttress to the peaceful ordering of society. They were discussing abolishing the monarchy (as the English had done in 1649, restoring it eleven years later). Traditional sexual morality was being abandoned, couples choosing to live together in loose unions rather than to marry, divorce being made easy for those who were already married, adultery and sexual experimentation of all sorts being redefined as progressive and advanced rather than immoral.

And with such extreme ideas entering mainstream thought, it was only a short step to arrive at the point of view that the notion of private property was wrong, that all the world's wealth should be shared in common. In this utopian vision there would no longer be distinctions between rich and poor, powerful and powerless, high class and low class. All would have enough—but none would have more than enough, and having more than enough, indeed having flamboyantly more than enough, was the principal goal of the capital's well-to-do.

It was all very alarming, this ferment of thought; doctors noticed an increase in their patients' attacks of asthma and stomach pain, hives and headaches—all symptoms of severe stress. A nightmarish vision arose to haunt many a sleepless night, a vision of the disenfranchised of England rising up en masse to slaughter the rich, just as the French peasants had risen up during the Great Fear of 1789 to burn the châteaux of their feudal overlords and massacre all those inside. Londoners became suspicious of their servants, of laborers working in their gardens or homes or passing in the street. Were they infected with the virus of equality from France? Would they try to bring revolution to England?

Most of all, property owners were uneasy about crime, and the ever-growing population of criminals. In recent years the number of crimes seemed to increase alarmingly, until the jails and prisons were overflowing with inmates. The large and formidable Newgate Prison, built during the 1770s, with its graceful Palladian façade, high thick walls and solid masonry, was a bastion of security in insecure times, a symbol, to Londoners, that the authority of the state was more potent than the advancing tide of criminality. In its outer courtyard malefactors were hanged, one after another, sometimes twenty or more in a single afternoon. Spectators by the thousands came to watch these "Hanging Matches," sitting in the capacious wooden grandstands that offered an unobstructed view of the platform and gallows, or looking on from the windows of their carriages, or standing in noisy clusters behind the guardsmen and mounted soldiers who ringed the place of execution.

To this grim place, Newgate Prison, Mary Bryant was brought in the last week of June, 1792, with her four

companions from Port Jackson, and on July 7 she was formally ordered "to remain on her former sentence, until she
should be discharged by due course of law."[1] Mary's "former sentence" was death. That the sentence would be carried
out "in due course of law" she surely had no doubt. The
only uncertainty was when.

The immensity of London, its din and grime, noise and
energy must have seemed overwhelming to Mary, accustomed to the villages and small market towns of Cornwall
and the town-size penal colony of Sydney Cove. When she
and James Martin, Nate Lilley, Will Allen and John Butcher
were brought before the magistrate Nicholas Bond to be
examined at the Sessions House in the Old Bailey, it must
have seemed as if much of London's energy and din were
brought into the courtroom, for a very large and noisy
crowd was waiting to see the prisoners.

If Mary was at all abashed by the sight of so many staring spectators, gawking and pointing at her and her companions, the better-dressed among the onlookers peering
quizzically at her through lorgnettes, the gentlemen holding
the scented tips of their canes to their noses to counteract the
stench of jail fever that permeated the room, she did not
betray any nervousness. Her demeanor outwardly calm, perhaps with a hint of defiance, she stood before the magistrate
in plain prison garb—the first clean, whole garments she
had worn in several years—her brown hair washed and
brushed, her face and hands scrubbed with coarse soap and
laved with water drawn from the river. She was twenty-seven
years old, but must have looked older. Her voice, when she
spoke, was clear, her answers to Nicholas Bond's questions
intelligent—or at any rate, more intelligent than the magistrate expected the answers of a woman condemned for highway robbery to be.

All of the convicts were questioned, each in turn giving an account of his or her experiences in the penal colony, the circumstances leading up to the escape from Sydney Cove, the long voyage in the open boat, the clashes with the aboriginal tribes, the events in Kupang and Timor and finally the long voyage back to London. It was an epic tale, an undeniably heroic tale, told from five different points of view. The spectators grew quiet when hearing of starvation in the colony, of the malarial plague in Timor, of the deaths of Will Morton and Sam Bird and the disappearance of James Cox and in particular of the deaths of Will Bryant and Mary's two children.

It was Mary's testimony that kept the large and unruly audience exceptionally quiet. The "woman question" was so much at issue just then, the political and social emancipation of women such a topic of heated debate. And here, in the flesh, was a woman to be reckoned with. A condemned criminal, hardened and guilty of serious wrongdoing and deserving of execution, and yet a woman of such grit, steel and courage that she had been able to endure hunger and illness and great danger and terrible loss—when Mary described the deaths of Charlotte and Emanuel many in the courtroom must have wept openly—and had not succumbed. Surely it would be difficult to find a more stalwart woman in all England, or one more deserving of the leniency of the court. For had she not, in her suffering and her heroism, paid for her crimes? Was she not deserving of a second chance, and her companions with her? And had she not said, in response to Nicholas Bond's questions, that she was sorry for having robbed Agnes Lakeman on the Exeter road six years earlier?

A collection was taken for Mary and her fellow prisoners, the clink of coins audible in the room as the magistrate brought the proceedings to a close. Cash was vital in prison;

with it a prisoner could pay the fees the jailers demanded and could buy the right to wear lighter chains, to have blankets, to have food sent in from outside to supplement the small chunk of bread that was the standard daily ration. These five prisoners would find their incarceration much easier with the funds the onlookers supplied.

All eyes were on Nicholas Bond as he announced his decision to the crowded courtroom. The prisoners were not to be committed for trial on the charge of escaping from captivity in New Holland. They were to remain in Newgate, awaiting "discharge by due course of law." They were all under sentence of death. But they had all plead their case, and won over the crowd. In the courtroom that day, for the space of a few hours, they had seemed, not criminals, but admired celebrities, Mary most of all.

XIX

I N THE COURTROOM on that warm July day in 1792 was
a bright-eyed, round-faced, double-chinned Scots gen-
tleman in a grey bag wig who followed the proceedings
with avidity. He was fifty-two years old and a barrister himself, moderately successful at the Scottish bar, though largely
idle since being called to the English bar six years earlier. And
he was a celebrity in the literary world of London: his
recently published biography of Samuel Johnson was a best-
seller and was receiving wide and generous praise.

He was the well-known, well-liked, vivacious and enter-
taining James Boswell, lord of Auchinleck, friend of King
George (who had been told by Edmund Burke that Boswell's
Life of Johnson was the most interesting book he had ever
read) and favorite guest at fashionable dinner parties. Sitting
in the magistrate's court, keenly attentive to the compelling
demeanor and riveting testimony of Mary Bryant and her

fellow convicts, all Boswell's natural gifts and talents were brought into sharpened focus: his penetrating eye, his boundless curiosity about the lives of others, his deep warmth of feeling, his strong sense of the pathetic.

He was entranced, especially by the clear-voiced Cornishwoman who showed such sturdy self-possession under the magistrate's questioning, even though aware that she stood under sentence of death. What an ordeal she had been through! What mental strain she must be under! Boswell's imagination was fully engaged; he could see in his mind's eye the unfolding drama of Mary's life, as she described it. The bleak impoverished childhood in Fowey, the days of outlaw daring and thievery, the wretchedness of imprisonment, the months at sea—every episode began to play itself out in his mental vision, as in a theatrical spectacle or a vivid novel. And here was the heroine of the novel, still a youngish woman, a woman triply bereaved yet able to face what remained of her life with composure.

Not only was Boswell impressed, he was drawn out of himself. Seized with Mary's story, taken with her plight, he forgot, for the moment, the darker threads of his own life, his recent deep depression ("perpetually gnawed by a kind of mental fever," as he put it), his all but desperate financial situation, his own bereavement—his wife Margaret had died three years earlier—his restlessness and nagging sense of personal dissatisfaction. Setting aside these preoccupations, he began to take action on Mary's behalf.

First, he collected seventeen guineas—a substantial amount—for her support while in prison. He would probably have offered to serve as her barrister if there had been a trial. But no trial was set; instead the government, in a quandary about how to treat the five increasingly celebrated escapees from New Holland, chose to simply delay and do nothing. To execute the five, in accordance with their original sentences, or to try them for escaping from transportation and sentence them to death, was impractical, for they had aroused so much admiration and sympathy that the public was solidly behind them. To execute them would bring unending criticism. Yet to pardon the five would be tantamount to condoning escape, which the court could not appear to do.[1]

Boswell's only recourse was to try to obtain a pardon for Mary, using his influence and his many government connections.

By good fortune Boswell was a very old acquaintance of the Secretary of State for the Home Department, Henry Dundas. As boys Boswell and Dundas had gone to college together (Boswell enrolled at the University of Edinburgh at thirteen), as barristers they had fought legal battles against one another in court, and Boswell had watched, in some amazement, as the hardheaded, blunt-spoken Dundas rose higher and higher in government service until he reached his present eminence. All was not harmonious between them; at school Boswell had been contemptuous of the intellectually plodding Dundas, and in later years Dundas was condescending and slighting to Boswell. Still, Boswell was prepared to overlook any risk of further insult to himself in the interest of helping Mary, and so he wrote to Dundas requesting a meeting. A time was agreed on, and Boswell presented himself on the appointed day—only to be left waiting. The great Dundas, perhaps genuinely overbooked, perhaps delivering a deliberate slight, did not appear.

"Dear Sir," Boswell wrote on the following morning,

> I stayed in town a day longer, on purpose to wait on you at your office yesterday about one o'clock, as your letter to

me appointed; and I was there a few minutes before one, but you were not to be seen.

The only *solatium* [consolation] you can give me for this unpleasant disappointment, is to favor me with two lines directed Penrhyn Cornwall* assuring me that nothing harsh shall be done to the unfortunate adventurers from New South Wales, for whom I interest myself, and whose very extraordinary case surely will not found a precedent.

A negative promise from a Secretary of State I hope will not be withheld, especially when you are the secretary, and the request is for compassion.

I always am, dear Sir, very faithfully yours,

James Boswell[2]

Boswell's efforts did not stop with Dundas. He also wrote to the Under-Secretary of State Evan Nepean, whose direct involvement with the planning and establishing of the colony at Sydney Cove was well known, and to the Chief Clerk in Dundas's office, William Pollock, who could be counted on to read any letter to Dundas that Dundas chose to ignore, and to give a response.

A response came: Mr. Henry Dundas agreed to "duly consider" Mr. Boswell's letter on behalf of the "Botany Bay prisoners." It was a cold reply—but at least it was a reply. For the moment, Mary was safe from further prosecution.

Mary was safe: in fact, Mary was vastly contented. To be sure, she might be executed, some time in the future. But for the present, she was comfortable, even luxuriant. According to one of the journalists who interviewed the five convicts

---

*Boswell was about to leave on a Cornish vacation, to visit his friend William Temple.

from New Holland they declared Newgate to be a "paradise" compared to the conditions under which they had been living for many years past.

And indeed it was a paradise of sorts. Even though crowded (in some small cells upwards of twenty men were living cheek by jowl), the prison in summer was warm and dry and, because it was relatively new, there was none of the pungent reek of centuries of decay and human neglect. Drink flowed freely—the prison keeper operated a tavern—and thanks to the public subscription taken up on her behalf, Mary was able to afford beer and probably gin as well.[3]

Debtors, of whom there were many imprisoned in Newgate, held banquets and soirées and even dances several times a week in their cells. Colorful prisoners gathered an audience of fellow convicts and recounted their exploits, or told of earlier inhabitants of London prisons who had led romantic lives. In her long, idle days in the summer of 1792, as she waited for further word from the magistrate or from her well-wisher Mr. Boswell, Mary must have heard stories of the highwayman James Maclean, "the Ladies' Hero," who had posed as an Irish squire with expensive lodgings in St. James's and who robbed coaches and carriages "with the greatest good breeding" until caught and hanged. And of murderous madmen who killed their servants or close relatives, or who, like the notorious Elizabeth Brownrigg, hired orphans from the Foundling Hospital only to chain them up like dogs and torture them to death.

There were tales of young girls who, before their capture, joined gangs of thieves and wandered through the crowds at theaters or outdoor markets or even open-air revival meetings, stealing purses and valuables. Some of the girls, practiced at deceit, put on pairs of false arms, which they kept modestly folded in front of them while with their real arms, concealed under their cloaks, they picked pockets.

These convict tales may have had a familiar ring to Mary, who by this time had spent much of her life in the company of criminals, and who may have known many a deceitful trick herself. One line of conversation must have fascinated her, however: talk of escape.

It was possible, escape from Newgate. It had been done. One condemned murderer had even escaped twice, while awaiting execution. The first time he had used a file, smuggled in to him without the guards' noticing, and had broken the bars on his cell window. Recaptured, he had escaped a second time by climbing a chimney and getting away over the rooftop.

If escape failed or was impracticable, there was the possibility of rescue. Only twelve years earlier rioting Londoners had broken into Newgate, set the prison on fire, and released five prisoners. It might easily happen again.

In the meantime all Mary could do was wait, with James and Will, Nate and John, all of whom were becoming more celebrated by the day. There were long articles about the five in the *London Chronicle* and *Irish Times*. James was dictating his own account of the daring escape from Sydney Cove, which he called *Memorandoms* and which would eventually become the only surviving firsthand record of the escapees' experiences.[4] Possibly others were telling their story to amanuenses or eager journalists. For a few brief months, the Botany Bay convicts, and especially Mary, the "Girl from Botany Bay," were the objects of intense curiosity and attention.

All the while, however, their fellow prisoners were succumbing to the harsh rigors of the Newgate jailers. Every day Mary witnessed floggings, and saw recalcitrant convicts burnt with branding irons and forced to walk for hours at a time on the dreaded treadmill—an exhausting torture that required the sufferer to walk continuously uphill along a moving wheel until every muscle was painfully cramped and every step an agony. Prisoners not yet put on trial were taken into the Sessions chamber courtyard and made to lie on the ground while heavy iron weights were piled onto their stomachs and chests until they agreed to plead guilty. If they were tough enough to withstand the pain of the weights, the ultimate torture was applied: the Skull Cap. Fettered to a stone wall, the hapless prisoner had an iron band fastened so tightly around his temples that he bled from his nose and ears. The band was tightened more and more cruelly until he begged for mercy—and agreed to plead guilty.

Surrounded by such terrible reminders of where she was and under what sentence she lay, yet enjoying her daily comforts in the interim, Mary passed ten months, from July of 1792 to the end of April, 1793.

Then, on May 2, came the sudden news of her release.

A free pardon had been granted. Boswell's appeals to Henry Dundas had borne fruit.

"Whereas Mary Bryant, otherwise Broad, now a prisoner in Newgate, stands charged with escaping from the persons having legal custody of her," the official document read, "[and] whereas some favorable circumstances have been humbly represented to us in her behalf inducing us to extend our Grace and Mercy unto her, and to grant her our Free Pardon for her Said Crime, Our Will and Pleasure therefore is, that you cause her, the said Mary Bryant, otherwise Broad, to be forthwith discharged out of custody."[5]

A Free Pardon. And from the king himself, whose initials, G.R. for George Rex, were at the top of the impressive document with its official-looking seal.

Mary could not read her pardon, of course. But it was read to her—perhaps by the prison keeper, perhaps by Boswell. And it meant that right then, that day, she was free to go.

The heavy cell door was opened, and then the outer door to the prison courtyard, and finally the gatehouse door through which she stepped—with what tears and smiles and sheer disbelieving rapture—into the sunlight of freedom.

XX

*I*T WAS OVER. The long ordeal, the years of suffering and fear, the ceaseless struggle, the shame.

Mary the convict, the convicted criminal, was no more. Now she was Mary the free woman, pardoned by the king himself, reborn to a fresh start and a new life.

It must have taken days, perhaps even weeks, for Mary to arrive at a full sense of her transformation. Days and weeks during which, guided by her rescuer James Boswell, she moved into a rented room in a lodging house in Little Titchfield Street near where Boswell's brother David lived, and began to accustom herself to London life. Having an entire room to herself must have seemed a great luxury—and not only a room, with a fireplace and a carpet, a bed and sofa and chairs and tables, but a place to hang her clothes and cabinets to store her few possessions.

Thanks to Boswell's continuing effort to collect charitable contributions on her behalf, Mary was acquiring the accoutrements of gentility: some day dresses, a bonnet and shawl for when she went out, and well-made shoes, not the rough clogs of a countrywoman but leather shoes, to be worn over stockings, the shoes of a gentlewoman. Probably there were gloves for her rough hands, and ribbons to trim her dresses, and colored bands to bind up her dark hair, for these were in vogue in the spring of 1793 and no respectable woman would go out without banded hair, any more than she would go out wearing rouge on her lips and cheeks. ("Only the disgraceful French," it was said, went "rouged and hatless" in public.)

The contrast between Mary's former shabby, shapeless prison garb and her new finery was startling—and emblematic of the new world that was opening before her. It was impossible for Mary not to feel different in her new clothes, and living in her new lodgings, and most of all, enjoying her newfound freedom. She answered to no one but herself. There were no schedules to follow, no rules to heed. All London was before her; she could go where she liked, see whom she liked. The hours of her days were hers to spend— or squander. Each night she slept well, and long. Each day she ate well.

Gradually her hard edges began to soften, her musculature to relax. Her body filled out, the wariness in her grey eyes began to give way to a brighter look, one of greater peace and security.

All London was Mary's to explore. The Thames, its garbage-ridden waters reeking in the spring heat. The narrow streets and alleys with their tempting shop windows where everything from fragrant hot cross buns and pastries to anthologies of sermons to anti-earthquake pills were sold.

Such an overplus of goods of every sort must have tempted Mary, after so many years of deprivation, to overindulge. With the pocket money Boswell gave her out of the fund he collected, she bought sweets and trinkets and, more than likely, called at the neighborhood gin shops where a glass of Blue Ruin could be had for a penny.

Most likely she took a boat to Vauxhall Stairs and paid her shilling to be admitted to the twelve attractively landscaped acres of Vauxhall Gardens, where the visitor could walk for miles along well-tended paths that led through green arbors and among blooming rhododendrons and beds of roses and lilac and laburnum. As if in a dream she walked beneath immense triumphal arches and past imitation ruins of Roman temples, while in the distance a band played marches and dance tunes. At her leisure, she took tea in the Chinese pavilion and watched the passing parade of fashionably dressed patrons, hoping to see the king.

There was much to divert Mary in the first few weeks of her new life. The daily small dramas in the street—carriages overturning, arguments between cart drivers, the commotion and clatter of sheep and cattle being driven to the slaughterhouses of Smithfield. Cries of street vendors and sellers of news sheets kept her informed of the rapidly unfolding events in the larger world. Rumormongers spread tales and gossip. And in the capital's hundreds of coffeehouses, where people gathered to read the newspapers, all the talk was of the war with France and of the seemingly berserk and savage Parisians, who had taken over the government and executed King Louis and were massacring innocent priests and aristocrats.

Whether Mary took advantage of her early days of freedom to explore London, or stayed close to her room, we don't know. Her benefactor Boswell looked in on her often—in his journal he wrote that he assumed "a very attentive charge of her"—and was frequently in Titchfield Street to visit his brother, with whom he often dined.[1] Mary knew no one else, only her four companions from Sydney Cove who were still in prison. Boswell assured Mary that he was endeavoring to have the four men pardoned, but had not succeeded. Boswell, it would seem, was Mary's entire society in her earliest weeks of freedom.

But Boswell was exceptionally busy that spring, and may have had scant time to spend with the Girl from Botany Bay, as the newspapers called her. Not only did he have an important case in the courts (a case he lost on the day after Mary's release) but he was eagerly immersed in making travel plans.

Since February of 1793, Britain had joined her continental allies in waging war against revolutionary France. Boswell planned to leave in June for Holland "to pass some time with the combined armies." No doubt he planned to send back accounts of his experiences to be published in the newspapers. He was compiling a book of his travels, and given his wide repute as a literary figure and the great success of his *Life of Johnson*, the projected book was bound to have very bright commercial prospects.

Events had been moving quickly over the past few months. The French armies, having advanced rapidly eastward as far as Mainz and taken Bruges, Liège and Antwerp to the north, had recently fallen back and begun to retreat. The Austrians were besieging the frontier fortresses of Condé and Valenciennes. With France itself plagued by internal upheaval, counterrevolutionaries in charge of several provincial cities and civil war in the Vendée, it looked as though the revolutionary government might fall and the monarchy be re-established. Boswell was enthusiastically planning to put himself in the heart of all the ferment.

Nothing pleased him more, nothing lifted his perennially depressed spirits more than hurry, bustle and activity; he was at his most buoyant when pressed for time.

Throughout the first week of June, 1793, he wrote letters and called on officials and colleagues, and dined with those in a position to inform him about current conditions in Holland and Flanders. In his exuberance he drank too much (as he usually did), and suffered for it, but went on drinking too much day after day and night after night. On June 5, late at night, he was on his way home, swaying as he walked and clearly intoxicated. He was in Titchfield Street, probably coming home after dining with his brother.[2] Suddenly from out of the darkness men attacked him, knocking him down, beating him on the head and arms and stealing his money and his watch before they ran off.

Stunned, Boswell lay in the dirt, bleeding, until a young barrister came by and found him, alerting the night watchman and the neighborhood patrol. Together they carried the injured man home.

Boswell was fortunate; the attack could well have been fatal, as many such street attacks were. Even so, he was an invalid for weeks, while the deep cuts on his head and arms healed and his bruises and aches gradually subsided.

The assault and its aftermath were sobering, both literally and metaphorically. Boswell wrote to his close friend and severest critic William Temple that he looked on his mugging as a crisis in his life.

"I trust I shall henceforth be a sober, regular man," he wrote. "Your suggestion as to my being carried off in a state of intoxication is awful."[3] He felt humiliated as well as injured, and the combination depressed him.

"My being knocked down in the street and consequent illness . . . sunk my spirits," he wrote in his journal. He had no heart to resume his former life, and was in "much pain from feebleness" for the rest of the summer.[4] He abandoned his plans to go to the continent, his "military ardor quite extinguished." Weak and sore, ashamed of himself and distracted in mind, unable to focus, he limped through his days, doing his best to fulfill his obligations but subdued and often somber.

Mary too had grown more subdued. Her initial elation after her release from Newgate had spent itself, to be replaced by nagging feelings of emptiness and dread. She was free, well fed, well dressed, and enjoying every convenience, yet she didn't belong. Smoky, noisy, exciting London was not her home, and never could be. No doubt she grieved for her children, and thought of the family she had left behind so long ago in Fowey, when she began her wanton career of crime. Would they ever be able to accept her? She doubted it—or so she told Boswell.[5]

There were few respectable paths open to her: marriage, if the right man could be found; employment, probably in a factory or in domestic service; or emigration, perhaps to Canada or America. Some or all of these possibilities may have preoccupied her as London emptied during the dusty midsummer heat of August, the propertied classes leaving for their country homes in preparation for the fall shooting season.

It was during this exodus, on a hot Sunday, that a visitor called on Boswell. He was a Mr. Castel, a Cornishman, from Mary's town of Fowey and an acquaintance of Mary's relatives.[6] One of the relatives—Mr. Castel did not say which one—had sent him a letter asking him to call on the famous Mr. Boswell, who had taken Mary as his protégé. Castel said that he wanted to see Mary and send word back to her family as to how she was.

And beyond that, he said, he had two pieces of good news for her. First, that her sister Dolly was in London, working as a cook at an establishment in Bedford Square. And second, that her father, along with three or four others in the family, had received a large inheritance.

At this, Boswell must have felt a chill of alarm. Confidence men often tried to trick the gullible by telling them that a large sum of money was on its way to them. Was this Castel—if that was his real name—nothing more than an impostor, trying to take advantage of Mary?

Did he imagine that he could extort money from Boswell in some way, using the spurious legacy as collateral? Castel mentioned an improbably immense sum: three hundred thousand pounds (the equivalent of seventeen million pounds in 2003).

All Boswell's suspicions, his latent snobbery, his sense of class and privilege, were aroused. How dare this blackguard try to hoodwink him, taking advantage of his acquaintance with Mary's kin?

But when Boswell took Castel to see Mary (who did not recognize him), Boswell's suspicions began to abate. In talking with Mary it became clear that Castel was who he claimed to be, and did know the Broads fairly well; he recognized Mary, who must have felt a combination of happiness and trepidation at hearing that Dolly was living and working not far away, and that Castel wanted to bring her sister to Mary's room that very evening.

When Castel began to talk of the family inheritance, Mary was strangely unmoved, as Boswell noted in his journal. Perhaps she disbelieved him, as Boswell himself did. In any case, she showed good sense, her protector thought, in being "shy to him [Castel] and not being elated by the sound of the great fortune." Mary was no fool; she knew the sound of trickery when she heard it.[7]

Not wanting to leave Castel alone with Mary, Boswell escorted him out, and made sure he left the immediate neighborhood, walking with him a long way and then returning to Mary's lodging alone to talk with her. He warned her not to believe anything Castel had said until he proved his good faith by producing her sister. No doubt Mary did not need the warning; she was on her guard.

It must have been a very long afternoon. Mary was alone, Boswell had gone to church and then to dine with legal colleagues. Thoughts of Cornwall, and of the family she had not seen for so many years, must have tumbled over themselves in Mary's mind. How far could she trust what she had been told, if at all? Was Dolly really in London? And if so, why had she not come herself before this to tell Mary of the change in the family fortunes?

Chances are Dolly could not have read about Mary in the newspapers, for like Mary, she was probably illiterate. But she could have heard others talking of the Girl from Botany Bay, the Cornish highwaywoman named Mary Bryant. She might have wondered whether it was her sister. Or someone in the family, the same person who sent Mr. Castel to Boswell, could have gotten word to Dolly that Mary was back from New Holland, and freed from imprisonment.

Dolly's arrival in Little Titchfield Street put an end to all conjecture. There she stood, in Mary's doorway, joyful, incredulous, her eyes full of tears. It was indeed Dolly, thirty years old now, but still youthful and slender—as Boswell noted when he saw her afterwards—and above all affectionate.[8]

No doubt the two women embraced, and wept together, and sat talking for a long time, with the avuncular Mr. Castel looking on. Mary must have told Dolly of her long odyssey of prison, voyaging, escape and recapture. Of the husband she had had and lost, of her two beloved children, both now dead. Of the miracle worked by Mr. Boswell, who had arranged for her pardon and release.

The tears must have fallen freely as Mary told her story, for Dolly was warmhearted and empathetic (when he met her, Boswell noted her great "tenderness of heart") and her sympathy and concern would have melted any reserve or wariness Mary felt. When Boswell arrived later, he found the two still talking, Dolly telling him that she had been "in great concern" about Mary and "showing her the most tender affection."

The benison of Dolly's love must have warmed Mary and put some of her trepidation to rest. She had family again, she was embraced and not scorned. And just possibly, all that Castel had said was true. Just possibly, Mary would one day be rich beyond her wildest dreams.

XXI

*T*HE MONEY, IT SEEMS, had changed everything.

There was indeed an inheritance (though it cannot have been three hundred thousand pounds, or anywhere near that much), and Mary's aged father stood to receive a share. That made Mary and Dolly heiresses—assuming Mary's father did not disinherit her—and the fact that she would be an heiress sweetened her relatives in their attitude toward her.

Boswell received a letter from a woman he thought was another sister of Mary's in Fowey—most likely it was from Elizabeth Puckey, the wife of Mary's cousin Ned Puckey. The letter said that Mary would be "kindly received" if she returned home, and on the strength of this assurance, it was agreed that Mary would sail for Cornwall as soon as a passage could be arranged.[1]

There were other letters, from Mary's cousin Ned, asking Boswell for legal advice on how Mary might obtain a share of the inheritance directly, without having to wait for her father to die before receiving any of it. Whether Boswell was able to offer any advice toward that end is unknown.

For Mary to return home seemed the wisest course, but she continued to have doubts. And because of those doubts, her sailing was delayed.

Not until October 12 did she make her way, escorted by Boswell, to Beale's Wharf in Southwark where the vessel *Ann and Elizabeth* rocked at anchor, being readied to sail for Cornwall. Boswell had booked Mary's passage, and paid for it, and to calm her fears about her future he had promised to give her an annuity of ten pounds a year (a very comfortable income) "as long as she behaved herself well," so that if all did not go well for her in Fowey she could afford to go elsewhere and live independently.

She had nothing with her but one box, filled with her clothes and personal things. The one memento she had brought from Sydney Cove, some leaves for making the "sweet tea" the convicts had drunk, she gave to Boswell.[2] Earlier in the day he had memorialized Mary by writing out "her curious account" of her escape from Sydney Cove. The little memorandum was not long—only two pages—and it has not survived.

Dusk had fallen when the hackney coach made its way to Beale's Wharf, and Mary's box was unloaded and taken aboard the *Ann and Elizabeth*. All the passengers were to sleep on board that night, for the ship was to sail very early the following morning. The lanterns were lit in the wharfside tavern, and Mary and Boswell went in, sitting in the kitchen and then in the bar, warming themselves with wine and brandy.

For nearly two hours they talked, while sailors and passengers came and went, the tavern landlord and the master of the ship joining them in a glass of wine.[3]

Boswell gave Mary five pounds and a little change to take with her, and assured her that he would look after Dolly and try to find her a better position—he thought the work she had was too hard for her. He spoke optimistically of the four convicts still in Newgate. He had been to see them several times, and was continuing his campaign of letters and appeals to have them pardoned, confident that they would indeed be released soon. No doubt, in the course of their long conversation, Mary and Boswell promised to write to each other, though Mary would have to find someone to write her letters for her.

"She said her spirits were low," Boswell wrote in his journal about their last meeting. "She was sorry to leave me; she was sure her relations would not treat her well."

He replied that she had an obligation to visit her father, who was elderly, and her other relatives. And besides, he said, it might be true that her father had become rich, or would be soon.

He did what he could to raise her spirits, but Mary was clearly doleful. When Boswell left her, after seeing her safely to her cabin and saying a last good-bye, she must have wept. Once more, as so often in the past, she was on her own. She had been largely on her own, through good fortune and bad, for nearly half her life. Now she was once again off into the unknown, leaving behind the two people who had been kindest to her, Boswell and Dolly. She was leaving with the protection of Boswell's promise of financial support but was dubious about what lay in store for her in Fowey. She had known so many reversals of fortune that it was hard to believe security was possible. It was hard to believe it, that is, late at night when she was full of wine, and had just said a final farewell to her greatest benefactor.

The next morning, it is to be hoped, her spirits were brighter.

Dawn was breaking over the Thames as the *Ann and Elizabeth* sailed downriver, going out to sea with the morning tide. No doubt Mary was on deck to watch as the vessel slipped past the docks and out into the broad estuary. She had never before been on deck to watch an embarkation; always before she had been in the hold, in chains, unable to see the ocean or the sky.

Now, watching the land rush past, smelling the sharp salt air, feeling the ship move under her as it began to ride the broad swells, she must have remembered those earlier journeys, aboard the *Charlotte*, the *Rembang*, the *Horssen*, the *Gorgon*, and the nameless small cutter she had shared with Will and her children and the seven others.

As the *Ann and Elizabeth* turned to the southwest, hugging the coast, the breeze began to freshen, and Mary wrapped her shawl more tightly around her shoulders. It would be cold in Cornwall, a wet October cold that brought on rheums and fevers. She could only hope that, in her parents' house, with all the relatives and neighbors gathered to see the famous Mary Bryant, the Girl from Botany Bay, there would be a warm fire and bowls of strong punch to revive her, and strong welcoming arms to embrace her and take her back into the family fold. Certainly there would be many a story to tell and re-tell on the long winter nights to come.

Afterword

No one knows what became of Mary Bryant after she returned to Fowey in the fall of 1793. Early the following year Mary's cousin Ned Puckey wrote to Boswell to send him Mary's thanks for all his kindness to her, and the note was signed with her initials. Boswell sent Mary her allowance, and received an assurance that she was continuing to conduct herself properly and had not fallen back, as so many convicts did, into a life of crime.

There was no further word of the inheritance.

Then in May of 1795 Boswell died, and his heirs canceled Mary's annuity.

It is possible that Mary died at about the same time as her benefactor, either in an epidemic or of a recurrence of malaria. Or, since there is no record in Fowey or surrounding parishes of the deaths of either Mary or Dolly or their parents, it is possible that the entire family moved away.

A woman named Mary Bryant is listed in the parish records of another Cornish town, Breage, in October of

1807. This Mary Bryant married a man named Richard Thomas, and had a daughter, Mary Anne, in 1811 and another daughter, Elizabeth, in July of 1812. But by 1812 the Mary Bryant of our story would have been forty-seven years old, assuming she survived, and most women in eighteenth- and early nineteenth-century England did not live that long, let alone bear children at such an advanced age.

Very likely we will never know what became of Mary. Like Boswell's brief record of her journey, and Will Bryant's log from the voyage up the coast of New Holland, Mary simply vanished into the obscurity that cloaks most far-off things, especially the lives of women. In Australia Mary is known today as a heroine, to the rest of the world she is only a name, and a little-known name. Her remarkable story ends, for us, in a small Cornish town in 1794, in a time of war and a season of gathering darkness.

Notes

Chapter I

1. Mary's baptismal record in the parish church of Fowey reads: "Mary, daughter of William Broad, mariner, and Grace his wife, of Fowey, was baptized in this church on May 1st 1765 by Nicholas Cory, Vicar."

   The incident for which Mary was jailed was described in the Trial Book of the Western Circuit. She was accused of "feloniously assaulting Agnes Lakeman, spinster, on the King's Highway, putting her to corporeal fear and danger of her life on this said highway and violently taking from her person and against her will in the said highway of one silk bonnet (value 12d.) and other goods to the value of £11 11s. (her property)."

   In the margin opposite this notation was written, "Mary Braund—to be hanged," along with the fainter inscription "High Roby" [Highway Robbery]." Judith Cook, *To Brave Every Danger* (London: Macmillan, 1993), pp. 44–45.

The two other women captured along with Mary were Mary Haydon (aka Mary Shepherd) and Catherine Fryer.

2. English men and women in the eighteenth century perceived that crime was increasing, but as A. G. L. Shaw, in *Convicts and the Colonies: A Study of Penal Transportation from Great Britain and Ireland to Australia and Other Parts of the British Empire* (Irish Historical Press, 1998), p. 38, points out, their perception was distorted by an erroneous assumption that crime is an aberration, not an inevitable dimension of social life, and that in previous centuries England was crime-free.

   The enormous growth in population in the later eighteenth century, the relative anonymity of city life, the absence of a police force and the restlessness and tumultuousness of the populace all reinforced the assumption that lawlessness was rising. Whether or not the crime rate was increasing is impossible to say; the great increase in laws intended to punish criminals reflected the general fear of crime rather than any genuine increase.

   Another distorting factor, in the closing decades of the century, was the advance in humane sensibility, reflected in an upsurge of opposition to slavery, blood sports and cockfighting. A new moral sentiment was emerging that was quick to identify wickedness of all kinds and apt to exaggerate it.

Chapter II

1. Donald Thomas, *Henry Fielding* (New York, 1990), p. 305.

2. Ibid., p. 303.

3. According to the description in the Newgate Prison Register, James Martin was 5'9", with black hair, grey eyes and a sallow complexion. The *Dublin Chronicle* claimed that he was from Antrim.

4. Crimes punishable by whipping, imprisonment, confinement in the pillory or hard labor included stealing lead, arson, theft of letters, bigamy, manslaughter, and the solemnizing of a marriage in secret. Theft of a dead body, perjury, fraud, and the keeping of a bawdy house, on the other hand, were only misdemeanors. Shaw, pp. 26–28.

5. Since judges were known to take character into account when determining sentences, and since execution (and transportation for crime) were looked on as a way of getting rid of undesirable members of society, it might be presumed that Mary Broad was of ill repute—as she probably was.

6. *The Life and Adventures of John Nicol, Mariner,* ed. Tim Flannery (New York, 1997), p. 120.

7. Thomas, pp. 304, 301. Fielding described dishonest magistrates in London who brought all the human refuse of the streets into their courtrooms, then charged each of the accused a bail fee as an alternative to weeks or months of imprisonment while they waited to be tried.

   One Bow Street magistrate, Sir Thomas de Veil, maintained a private room where he took attractive female prisoners, settling their cases and then asking each woman "if she had not a back-door to her lodging, where a [sedan chair] might stop without suspicion?" and "when an amicable visit might be received without interception?"

8. The term "transportation" was first used in the reign of Charles II, in 1680. By the 1760s the usual term for a convict whose sentence had been commuted to transportation was fourteen years. Judges, having condemned prisoners to execution, recommended commutation of the sentence, and the king, after consulting with the home secretary, endorsed the judge's recommendation. James Martin, *Memorandoms*, ed. Charles Blount (Cambridge, 1937), pp. 9–10.

9. Shaw, pp. 46–48. Governor Phillip, in his account of the voyage to New Holland, implied that some convicts were

actually sent to Africa, with fatal results. He wrote that when transportation to America ceased to be feasible, "other expedients, well known to the public, have since been tried. . . . Particularly, the transporting of criminals to the coast of Africa, where what was meant as an alleviation of punishment too frequently ended in death." *The Voyage of Governor Phillip to Botany Bay; with an Account of the Establishment of the Colonies of Port Jackson and Norfolk Island* (London, 1789), p. 6.

10. When the voyage was planned, a proposal was put forward to bring a number of women from the Friendly Isles or New Caledonia to be sexual companions for the men, and so "preserve the settlement from gross irregularities and disorders." Frederick A. Pottle, *Boswell and the Girl from Botany Bay* (New York, 1937), p. 22.

11. The "youngest and handsomest of the women" were selected, according to a witness before the Select Committee on the State of Gaols in 1819. Anne Summers, *Damned Whores and God's Police* (Ringwood, Victoria, 1994), p. 315. In actuality, virtually all healthy women convicts under forty-five were transported. Margaret Weidenhofer, *The Convict Years* (Melbourne, 1973), p. 74.

    Governor Phillip's instructions, dated April 25, 1787, ordered him to supplement the women making the journey by taking aboard any other women encountered during the voyage "who may be disposed to accompany them to the said settlement." *Historical Records of Australia*, I, p. 14.

Chapter III

1. W. Branch-Johnson, *The English Prison Hulks* (London, 1957), p. 33, citing convict James Hardy Vaux.

2. Shaw, p. 164; Nicol, pp. 114ff.
3. Nicol, pp. 124–125.
4. Branch-Johnson, p. 34.
5. Ibid., p. 81.
6. Ibid., pp. 180–181.
7. Ibid., pp. 9–10, 31–32.

Chapter IV

1. The *Charlotte* transport was variously listed by the official registers as 335–345 tons. Charles Bateson, *The Convict Ships, 1787–1868* (Glasgow, 1959), p. 97.
2. Pottle, *Boswell*, p. 23. On March 12, two months before the departure of the fleet, Governor Phillip had written Lord Sydney (Thomas Townshend, First Baron Sydney, Home and Colonial Secretary and Governor Phillip's immediate superior) asking him to put Phillip on record as refusing responsibility for convict and crew deaths. Sydney was not unsympathetic; when Surgeon White appealed for fresh provisions for the convicts who were still in port, Sydney ordered wine and foodstuffs for the sick sent immediately.
3. Branch-Johnson, p. 62.
4. Pottle, *Boswell*, p. 23. "Some part of the clothing for the female convicts" remained undelivered at the time of sailing. Phillip, p. 12.
5. Bateson, p. 13.
6. Phillip, p. 12.
7. Bateson, p. 99.
8. Lieutenant King wrote in his journal that in the quarrel between the seamen and the masters, who had withheld

their pay, Commander Phillip backed the masters. Cited in *Journal of a Voyage to New South Wales by John White, Surgeon-General to the First Fleet and the Settlement at Port Jackson*, ed. Alec H. Chisholm (Sydney, 1962), p. 51.

9. Though no male convict named Spence is noted in the records of the First Fleet, there was a female convict named Mary Spence listed in Arthur Phillip's roll call of prisoners. Phillip, p. lxxi. Since Mary Broad's name is not on the governor's list, it is quite likely that "Mary Spence" is Mary Broad, listed as the "lag wife" of a convict or guard named Spence. There were also several male prisoners named Spencer; it is possible that one of these men was the father of Mary's child, and the official who made out baby Charlotte Spence's birth record left off the final "r" in the name.

10. Bateson, p. 116.

11. Ibid., p. 99. Even before the fleet sailed, five women on board the *Lady Penrhyn* were put in irons for prostitution, and the second mate was dismissed.

    Sex between women convicts and members of the crew tended, by the time the Second Fleet sailed to New South Wales, to become a matter of stable ongoing unions rather than a promiscuous free-for-all. John Nicol wrote how, on the Second Fleet ship *Lady Juliana*, "when we were fairly out to sea, every man on board took a wife from among the convicts, they nothing loath." Nicol, p. 121. By 1816 it had become customary for every sailor to take a female convict as his temporary wife, and to be allowed to live with her during the passage. Shaw, p. 125.

12. The two organizers of the mutiny were Phillip Farrell, a former boatswain's mate, and Thomas Griffiths, formerly master of a French privateer. White, p. 15.

13. Phillip, p. 15.

14. White, p. 54. "At length, by an artful petition he [Powell]

got written for him," White wrote, "he so wrought on the governor's humanity as to procure a release from his confinement."

Chapter V

1. White, p. 60. The crossing of the Tropic of Cancer took place on June 15, 1787. The convoy did not reach the equator until July 14, but observed the traditional ceremony a month early.

2. A convict who lived through the sweltering heat of the doldrums, John Boyle O'Reilly, described the ordeal in his novel *Moondyne*. "The air was stifling and oppressive. There was no draught through the barred hatches. The deck above them was blazing hot. The pitch dropped from the seams, and burned their flesh as it fell. There was only one word spoken or thought—one yearning idea in every mind—water, cool water to slake the parching thirst . . ." Cited in Bateson, p. 72.

3. White, p. 63.

4. Ibid., p. 69. White gives a date of July 30 for this accident. Other accounts date it toward the end of May.

5. Ibid., pp. 70–71. Surgeon White was impressed with the ingenuity of the convicts, some of whom were professional counterfeiters, in creating high-quality imitation coins under conditions in which they were closely supervised by guards, never allowed to have fires, or artfully hid their apparatus. "The adroitness . . . with which they must have managed," White wrote, "in order to complete a business that required so complicated a process, gave me a high opinion of their ingenuity, cunning, caution, and address."

6. The convict James Hardy Vaux described how the guards, sadistic and cruel and bestial in their natures, carried

"large and ponderous sticks, with which, without provocation, they beat the convicts, "frequently repeating their blows long after the poor sufferer is insensible." Cited in Branch-Johnson, p. 33. Some prisoners aboard the hulks confided to an inspector that, having been "penned up like so many dirty hogs," all that kept them from despair was "one hope of revenge." Branch-Johnson, p. 76.

7. White, p. 88.

Chapter VI

1. During November the convoy covered more than 1,650 miles in sixteen days, an average of 103-plus miles a day. White, pp. 242–243. Scurvy struck the *Charlotte* in mid-December, "mostly among those who had the dysentery to a violent degree." Surgeon White wrote in his journal that he was "pretty well able to keep it under by a liberal use of the essence of malt and some good wine." Ibid., pp. 103–104.

2. Cited in White, p. 243.

3. Phillip, v. The *Sirius* sighted land at noon on January 3, 1788.

Chapter VII

1. Phillip, pp. 45–46.

2. Bateson, p. 115.

3. Phillip, p. 47.

4. White, p. 249.

5. Flies in Port Jackson were "so troublesome . . . that no fanning will keep them from coming to one's face; and without the assistance of both hands to keep them off,

they will creep into one's nostrils, and mouth too, if the lips are not shut very close." Watkin Tench, *Sydney's First Four Years. Being a reprint of A Narrative of the Expedition to Botany Bay and A Complete Account of the Settlement at Port Jackson* (Sydney, 1961), p. 103, editor's note.

6. Cook, p. 112, cites an instance of two men who lay in wait for women coming from bathing; one of the men was discovered grappling with his half naked victim on the ground and the women's companions struggled to free her.

7. Cited in Tench, pp. 98–99; Clark, *Journal*, cited in Cook, p. 111.

8. "The very small proportion of females makes the sending of an additional number absolutely necessary," Phillip wrote to Lord Sydney in England. Summers, p. 314.

9. Clark, *Journal*, cited in Cook, p. 111.

10. Ibid.

11. David Collins wrote in his journal that "Bryant has been frequently heard to express, what was indeed the general sentiment on the subject among the people of his description, that he did not consider his marriage in this country as binding." Captain David Collins, *An Account of the English Colony in New South Wales*, ed. James Collier (Christchurch, Wellington and Dunedin, New Zealand, Melbourne, and London, 1910), p. 114.

12. Cook, p. 104, citing Clark, *Journal*, February 11, 1788.

13. White, pp. 247–248.

Chapter VIII

1. Cook, p. 114.

2. Tench, p. 133.

3. White, p. 298. Surgeon White recorded forty-eight deaths: three marines, two marines' children, twenty-two male convicts, eight female convicts, nine convicts' children, four people executed. But Tench's record was fifty-four convict deaths ("including the executions"), plus one sergeant and two privates, for a total of fifty-seven. Tench, p. 72.

4. Tench, pp. 44, 100–101.

5. Collins, p. 44.

6. Born in either 1762 or 1763, Will may have been the William Bryant whose birth was recorded in Launceston in July of 1762. Cook, p. 26. Although Surgeon White thought Bryant was of good character, Judge Advocate Collins disagreed.

    Writing of those convicts singled out to "instruct and direct others in the exercise of professions," Collins wrote that some "had given evident proofs, or strong indications of returning dispositions to honest industry. There were others, however, who had no claim to this praise. Among those must be particularized William Bryant. . . . He was detected in secreting and selling large quantities of fish, a practice which he had pursued from his first appointment." Collins, pp. 44–45.

7. Pottle, *Boswell,* p. 24. William Bryant was sentenced at the Launceston Assizes in 1784 to seven years' transportation "for resisting the Revenue officers, who attempted to seize some smuggled property he had." He was convicted of forgery, for using the name Timothy Cary. Cook, p. 38.

    Phillip, p. lvii, lists William Bryant as having been convicted at Launceston on March 20, 1784. The *London Chronicle* of June 30–July 3, 1792, recorded that Will had been convicted "6 1/2 years ago" at Bodmin, which would have put his conviction at the end of 1786 or early 1787.

8. White, pp. 247–248; Collins, p. 21. In February, 1788, the month of Will and Mary's wedding, eighteen other couples

were married, including three couples wed alongside the Bryants on February 10.

9. Tench, pp. 145, 305. Duelling between Assistant Surgeon William Balmain and Surgeon-General John White in August of 1788 was the outcome of a quarrel fomented by the troublemaking marines.

10. Ibid.

11. Details of the celebrations are in Tench, pp. 60–61, and White, pp. 140, 256.

12. White, pp. 253–254. Despite the governor's announcement, from June 17, 1788 on he referred in writing to the settlement as "Sydney."

13. Ibid., p. 141.

Chapter IX

1. What became of the two who did not return, Ann Smith and Peter Paris, is not known for certain. La Pérouse denied having given any of the convicts refuge on his ship, but he may have been disingenuous, or his crew may have concealed the convicts aboard without his knowledge. According to what the returned escapees said, Ann Smith and Peter Paris lost their way and died of starvation. White, pp. 114–115.

2. Tench, p. 107. Tench's editor refers to the "prevailing belief" that the two convicts had managed to escape successfully, probably with La Pérouse's company.

3. Ibid., p. 137.

4. White, p. 142.

5. When Mary and her party of escapees reached the far northern part of the Australian continent, they reportedly encountered a group of aboriginals who used bows and arrows. Martin, p. 34.

6. Tench, pp. 46–49, 104–105, 137.

7. Ibid., p. 49.

8. Ibid., p. 50. The two murders occurred on May 30, 1788, the assault and abduction on May 21. The severed head seen by Edward Corbett probably belonged to the abductee, Peter Burn.

9. Ibid., pp. 55, 107.

10. Ibid., pp. 50–52.

11. White, p. 154; Tench, p. 136.

12. Tench, p. 287.

13. Ibid., p. 59.

14. Judge Advocate Collins, as noted earlier, was in no doubt that Will had "secreted and sold" large quantities of fish "from his first appointment," and that he was not trustworthy. Collins, pp. 44–45. Surgeon White, however, was a character witness for Bryant at his trial for theft, swearing that he had been trustworthy when on the *Charlotte*.

    But the surgeon was of an overly sanguine disposition, inclined to see the best in people and situations, as his journal frequently reveals. A clever opportunist and con man could have convinced White of his honesty while actually carrying on a brisk illegal trade. It is worth noting that when William Bryant went on trial for stealing fish, only the surgeon spoke up on his behalf; there was no general clamor that he was innocent.

15. Joseph Paget is listed as a prisoner, convicted at Exeter Assizes on January 10, 1786, and sentenced to seven years' transportation. Phillip, p. lxviii.

Chapter X

1. Vaccination, which ultimately eradicated smallpox (except in laboratory samples) in our time, was not begun in

England until the late 1790s, nearly a decade after the founding of Port Jackson. Tench, pp. 146–147ff, 306, described the smallpox epidemic among the aboriginal people. Only one of the newcomers came down with the disease, and he was not a European, but a Native American, a seaman aboard the *Supply*.

Tench was puzzled about how smallpox could have arisen among the aboriginal people but did note that "our surgeons had brought out variolous matter in bottles"—that is, the smallpox germ. "But," he added, "to infer that it [the smallpox] was produced from this cause were a supposition so wild as to be unworthy of consideration." Tench, p. 146.

2. Tench, p. 149.

3. Collins, p. 114.

4. According to Phillip, p. lvii, William Bryant was sentenced to seven years' transportation at Launceston on March 20, 1784. The *London Chronicle* of June 30–July 2, 1792, said that Will was convicted "six and a half years ago"—that is, at the end of 1786 or early 1787, at Bodmin.

5. Tench, p. 305.

6. Tench, p. 309.

7. Shaw, p. 73.

8. The weekly sailings from Port Jackson to Botany Bay ended in July, 1789. Tench, p. 162.

9. Tench, p. 272.

10. Ibid., pp. 162–163.

Chapter XI

1. Tench, p. 166.

2. Ibid., pp. 162–163.

3. Shaw, p. 115. The *Guardian* sank on December 23, 1789. With her was lost, besides her crew and officers, £70,000 worth of food stores, livestock and plants.

4. Tench, p. 165.

5. Collins, p. 82, wrote that during the entire first half of May 1790 the fishermen brought in less than 2,000 pounds.

6. Tench, pp. 167, 311.

7. Martin is described in the MS Registers of Newgate Prison, 1792–1793 as "age thirty-four [in 1792], height 5'9", grey eyes, black hair, sallow complexion, born in Ireland." Pottle, *Boswell*, p. 47. He was convicted at Exeter Assizes and sentenced on March 20, 1786, to seven years' transportation. Phillip, p. lxvii. *Evening Mail*, June 29–July 2, 1792.

   It was Martin whose *Memorandoms* provide the most valuable surviving record of the escape from Port Jackson, and who had the strength and initiative to ingratiate himself with the Dutch officials on Timor, earning a large sum of money for his labors and paying for his room and board before he and the rest of the escapees were taken into custody.

8. Captain Edwards considered Cox to be equally responsible with the Bryants in planning the escape. Edward Edwards, *Voyage of the HMS* Pandora, ed. Basil Thomson (London, 1915), p. 82.

9. Tench, p. 169.

10. In actuality La Pérouse and his ships had been lost at sea.

11. Tench, pp. 322–323.

Chapter XII

1. Bateson, p. 129, citing Reverend Richard Johnson.

2. Tench had alluded to the "incredible severity" with which

the Second Fleeters had been treated during their voyage—far worse than anything the First Fleeters had experienced. The ship's master, Nicholas Anstis, deliberately reduced the food rations allotted to each convict in order to sell the uneaten portions for his own profit. Convicts were kept heavily ironed, shackled together, kept in the dim hold and rarely allowed to come up on deck.

Mortality was very high during the voyage, from starvation, scurvy and dysentery, and when convicts died, their corpses remained shackled to the living—a state of affairs actually welcomed by those who survived as it meant they could share the rations allotted to the dead.

On the small *Surprize*, a "wet ship," the convicts were "considerably above their waists in water" when the seas were rough. Men with berths in the rear of the ship were "nearly up to the middles." Bateson, pp. 127–128.

The contrast between the sufferings of the convicts aboard the *Surprize*, *Neptune* and *Scarborough* and the relatively good treatment of the women aboard the *Lady Juliana* and the crew of the transport *Justinian* is startling. Mortality aboard the *Lady Juliana* was relatively low, and the *Justinian* brought her entire crew into harbor, from Falmouth, in five months without any sickness on board whatsoever. Tench, p. 172.

3. Nicol, p. 119.

4. Bateson, pp. 128–129.

5. Collins, p. 95, wrote that "information having been received the several convicts proposed making their escape from the colony in [the *Neptune*], the governor sent an armed party of soldiers to search the ship, when two men and one woman were found concealed among the firewood. They were taken on shore, and the men punished for their attempt."

6. The escape is described in Tench, pp. 181–182 and 316, citing Collins. There were five escapees, all men, but one

died. The other four were discovered and picked up in 1795 at Port Stephens, where they were living among the aboriginal people.

7. Pottle, *Boswell,* pp. 48–49.

8. John Butcher, who used the aliases William Butcher, Samuel Broome and John Brown, was incorrectly described by Pottle, *Boswell,* p. 48, as having been on the First Fleet.

   After his release Butcher wrote to Home Secretary Henry Dundas offering to return to Sydney Cove as a free settler, and pointing out his usefulness to the colony as an expert farmer. When no response was forthcoming Butcher enlisted as a private in the New South Wales Corps, returned to Sydney Cove, and was eventually given a twenty-five-acre farm at Petersham Hill in 1795. Cook, p. 240.

9. The terrible harm done by "Batavian fever," or malaria, was unmistakable; when the *Waaksamheyd* arrived from Batavia in December of 1790, it carried a midshipman named Ormsby who had caught the fever and eventually recovered. He was, Collins wrote, "the living picture of the ravages made in a good constitution by a Batavian fever." Collins, p. 144, cited in Tench, p. 321.

10. Tench, p. 220.

Chapter XIII

1. James Martin, in his *Memorandoms*, wrote that the escape party had an "open six-oar boat" with a hundredweight of flour, another hundred pounds of rice—probably the weevil-infested rice Captain Smith had brought from Batavia—along with fourteen pounds of pork and about eight gallons of water. Martin also says they had a compass, quadrant and chart.

   Contemporary and secondary sources vary in their

statements about the equipment and resources the Bryants and their fellow escapees had, and the sources of each of these items. I have attempted to reconcile these varying accounts, and to follow the most reliable of them.

It is greatly to be regretted that the memoir written by William Bryant of the journey he and Mary and the others took from Sydney Cove to Queensland has not survived. William Bligh read Bryant's memoir in manuscript, and made an attempt to have it copied, but only Bligh's recorded recollections of it survive, nothing of the text itself.

2. Cook, pp. 149–150. The accident was witnessed by Captain Hunter, who had been in command of the *Sirius* when it was wrecked.

Chapter XIV

1. Martin, p. 20.
2. Ibid., pp. 21–22.
3. Ibid., p. 25.
4. Ibid.
5. Ibid., pp. 25–26.
6. Ibid., p. 28.
7. Ibid., p. 29.
8. Ibid., p. 32.

Chapter XV

1. Martin, p. 32.
2. Ibid., p. 36.

3. "We remained very happy at our work, for two months," James Martin wrote, "until William Bryant had words with his wife and informed against himself, wife and children and all of us." Martin, p. 37.

Chapter XVI

1. Martin, p. 37.
2. In his memoir of the escape from Port Jackson and its aftermath, James Martin wrote that William Bryant's revelation of the convicts' true identity came two months after their arrival in Kupang. Since they arrived on June 6, 1791, this would put Bryant's confession and the convicts' immediate imprisonment in August. Martin, p. 37.

   Captain Edwards and the remnant of his crew and passengers did not arrive in Kupang until September 15, by which time Mary and Will and the others had been in the castle dungeon for a month or more.

   Cook, in *To Brave Every Danger*, pp. 171ff, speculates, departing from Martin's clear chronology, that it was the arrival of Edwards that led to Will Bryant's admission and the subsequent imprisonment of the Port Jackson convicts. But this is an unwarranted embroidery on the slender but unambiguous contemporary evidence.

Chapter XVII

1. Mary, Charlotte and Will Allen sailed on the *Horssen*. James Martin, Nate Lilley and John Butcher sailed on the *Hoornwey*, along with the two convicts who died on the voyage, Will Morton and Sam Bird.
2. Martin, pp. 39–40.

Chapter XVIII

1. James Martin wrote that "We was brought ashore at Purfleet and from there conveyed by the constable to Bow Street office, London, and was take to Justice Bond and was fully committed to Newgate." p. 40.

Chapter XIX

1. Evan Nepean, Under Secretary at the Home Office, told Boswell that "Government would not treat [Mary and the four men] with harshness, but at the same time would not do a kind thing to them, as that might give encouragement to others to escape." Pottle, *Boswell,* p. 36.

2. Pottle, *Boswell,* facing p. 36, reproduction of holograph.

3. Though a 1751 Act of Parliament prohibited the sale of spirits in prisons, the law was not enforced and prison keepers were usually publicans; in some small prisons, convicts drank alongside tavern customers from off the street, and the two groups played skittles together. M. Dorothy George, *London Life in the Eighteenth Century* (New York, 1965), pp. 300–301. In the King's Bench prison, there were said to be thirty gin shops.

4. As noted earlier, Will Bryant kept a log of the escape journey, but it has not survived.

5. Pottle, *Boswell,* p. 54, citing Public Record Office, Correspondence and Warrants, Entry Book, H.O. 13/9f. p. 221; Newgate Register H.I. 26/56, p. 57.

Chapter XX

1. James Boswell, *Papers, Journal,* Vol. 18, p. 194.

2. Boswell's brother David lived in Titchfield Street, Mary Bryant in Little Titchfield Street. On the night of his mugging, it is possible that Boswell was visiting Mary, but unlikely. Their relationship seems to have been entirely platonic and disinterested on Boswell's part; in his journal he writes of Mary in a quite different tone from the one he used to describe or allude to his many casual mistresses and the prostitutes he picked up in the street and in taverns. Possibly she rebuffed his attempts at seduction. Possibly he had scruples where Mary was concerned, or perhaps she didn't appeal to him. More likely the protective role he took toward her precluded any erotic liaison.

3. Frank Brady, *James Boswell: The Later Years, 1769–1795* (New York, Toronto and London, 1984), p. 477.

4. Boswell, *Papers, Journal,* Vol. 18, pp. 246, 203. Boswell was still complaining of severe pain at the end of August.

5. In October 1793 Mary told Boswell "she was sure her relations would not treat her well" once she returned to Fowey. Boswell, *Papers, Journal,* Vol. 18, p. 217.

6. The incident with Mr. Castel is described in detail in Boswell, *Papers, Journal,* Vol. 18, p. 200.

7. Ibid.

8. Boswell wrote of Dolly that she was "a very fine, sensible young woman, and of such tenderness of heart that she yet cried and held her sister's hand."

   Dolly was so slim and young-looking that Boswell took her to be much younger than she was, calling her "a fine girl of twenty." Boswell, *Papers, Journal,* Vol. 18, pp. 203, 200.

Chapter XXI

1. On August 25, 1793, Boswell wrote in his journal, "It was now fixed that Mary should go by the first vessel to Fowey

to visit her relations." Boswell, *Papers, Journal,* Vol. 18, p. 204.

2. Mary's relatives had promised to give Boswell a generous reward for all his efforts on Mary's behalf. The warm and generous Dolly Broad had "expressed herself very gratefully" to Boswell and told him that "if she got money as was said, she would give [him] a thousand pounds." Boswell, *Papers, Journal,* Vol. 18, p. 203. Mary echoed this sentiment. Ibid., p. 204.

3. Boswell's account of his leavetaking from Mary is in his *Journal,* Vol. 18, pp. 217–218.

A Note on Sources

Very little is known about Mary Bryant, and the contemporary records concerning her are few in number. The paucity of source material has invited earlier writers to greatly embroider and romanticize the known facts of Mary's story; the most recent of these writers, Judith Cook, in *To Brave Every Danger*, (London: Macmillan, 1993), cites no source references and invents freely, sometimes contradicting the written records.

In reconstructing the tale of Mary's adventures from her point of view, I have relied on the vast literature on eighteenth-century England, on the knowledge gained from my seven previous books on the eighteenth and early nineteenth centuries, and in particular on the following works cited in the notes:

Bateson, Charles. *The Convict Ships, 1787–1868*. Glasgow: Brown, Son and Ferguson, 1959.

Boswell, James. *Papers, Journal.* Vol. 18. New York: McGraw-Hill, 1950– .

Brady, Frank. *James Boswell: The Later Years, 1769–1795.* New York, Toronto and London: McGraw-Hill, 1984.

Branch-Johnson, W. *The English Prison Hulks.* London: Christopher Johnson, 1957.

Collins, Captain David. *An Account of the English Colony in New South Wales, 1788–1801.* Edited by James Collier. Christchurch: Wellington and Dunedin, New Zealand, Melbourne, and London: Whitcombe and Tombs, 1910.

Edwards, Captain Edward. *Voyage of the HMS Pandora.* Edited by Basil Thomson. London, 1915.

George, M. Dorothy. *London Life in the Eighteenth Century.* New York: Capricorn Books, 1965.

Martin, James. *Memorandoms.* Edited by Charles Blount. Cambridge, Eng.: Rampart Lions Press, 1937.

Nicol, John. *The Life and Adventures of John Nicol, Mariner.* Edited with an introduction by Tim Flannery. New York: Atlantic Monthly Press, 1997.

Phillip, Arthur. *The Voyage of Governor Phillip to Botany Bay; with an Account of the Establishment of the Colonies of Port Jackson and Norfolk Island.* London: John Stockdale, 1789.

Pottle, Frederick A. *Boswell and the Girl from Botany Bay.* New York: The Viking Press, 1937.

Shaw, A. G. L. *Convicts and the Colonies: A Study of Penal Transportation from Great Britain and Ireland to Australia and other parts of the British Empire.* Irish Historical Press, 1998.

Summers, Anne. *Damned Whores and God's Police.* Ringwood, Victoria Australia: Penguin Books, 1994.

Tench, Watkin. *Sydney's First Four Years. Being a reprint of A Narrative of the Expedition to Botany Bay and A*

Complete Account of the Settlement at Port Jackson. Sydney: Angus & Robertson, 1961.

Thomas, Donald. *Henry Fielding.* New York: St. Martin's Press, 1990.

Weidenhofer, Margaret. *The Convict Years.* Melbourne: Lansdowne Press, 1973.

White, John. *Journal of a Voyage to New South Wales by John White, Surgeon-General to the First Fleet and the Settlement at Port Jackson.* Edited by Alec H. Chisholm. Sydney: Angus & Robertson, 1962.

Index

vaccination, 208–9n.1
Van Diemen's Land (Tasmania),
    53, 55–56, 57
Vaux, James Hardy, 203–4n.6
Vauxhall Gardens, 183
venereal disease, 69
*Vindication of the Rights of
    Women, A* (Wollstonecraft),
    168

Waaksambeyd (Dutch supply
    ship), 116, 117–18, 122
Wanjon, Timotheus, 141, 148,
    194
water supply
    Bryant escape party, 119–20,
        123, 127, 128, 131, 132
    Horssen, 158
    Port Jackson contaminants,
        67, 68
    Rembang, 154
    transport convoy, 32, 43, 45,
        47, 52
Watson, Thomas, 16
White, John, 31–32, 37, 44,
    45, 65, 68, 73, 78, 88
    on birth of Mary's baby, 48

as Will Bryant's defender,
    83–84, 85
personal conflicts, 47, 91
Wollstonecraft, Mary, 168
woman question, 168
women agitators, 4
women convicts
    colorful tales of, 177–78
    convoy numbers, 30
    criminal offenses, 12, 13,
        23–24, 35
    escape plots of, 76
    escapes, 76, 110
    obstreperousness of, 22–23,
        35–36, 102
    penal colony sentence, 15–16
    Port Jackson deaths, 69
    Port Jackson lawlessness, 91
    scurvy victims, 52
    seaboard punishments, 63
    sexual use of, 15–16, 26–27,
        35, 61–63
    shipboard births, 43–44
    shipboard plight, 31, 35–36,
        43–44, 50, 52, 55
Worgan, Surgeon, 88
Wright, Henry, 91